Writer's 1-year Planner Journal

DESIGNED BY CAS FICK

First paperback edition January 2024

ISBN: 978-0-9950129-2-9

www.cmfick.com

Cas Fick Designs

For my Family

Note from the designer

I'm not very good at these sort of things, so I'll be brief. I hope that you use this journal as a starting place for organizing your writing time and as a place to jot down those notes that pop into your head while you're on the go. This planner can work for fiction and non fiction projects alike and is designed to help you organize and track your time.

By a writer for writers (and editors)

Instructions

There are no instructions! Grab your highlighters, your markers, and your washi tape, and utilize this book however best suits you. If you feel so inclined, please tag @cmfick on Instagram or @cm.fick on TikTok in any videos or pictures of your beautiful process using #MyPlannerJournal

In the back of this book you will find 12 months of color-matching tabs you can cut out and use with each corresponding month.

You can also find more 12-month printable tabs and a name plate at:

www.cmfick.com/printables

2024

January

S	M	T	W	T	F	S
	1	2	3	4	5	6
7	8	9	10	11	12	13
14	**15**	16	17	18	19	20
21	22	23	24	25	26	27
28	29	30	31			

February

S	M	T	W	T	F	S
				1	2	3
4	5	6	7	8	9	10
11	12	13	**14**	15	16	17
18	**19**	20	21	22	23	24
25	26	27	28	29		

March

S	M	T	W	T	F	S
					1	2
3	4	5	6	7	8	9
10	11	12	13	14	15	16
17	18	19	20	21	22	23
24	25	26	27	28	29	30
31						

April

S	M	T	W	T	F	S
	1	2	3	4	5	6
7	8	9	10	11	12	13
14	**15**	16	17	18	19	20
21	22	23	**24**	25	26	27
28	29	30				

May

S	M	T	W	T	F	S
			1	2	3	4
5	6	7	8	9	10	11
12	13	14	15	16	17	18
19	20	21	22	23	24	25
26	**27**	28	29	30	31	

June

S	M	T	W	T	F	S
						1
2	3	4	5	6	7	8
9	10	11	12	13	14	15
16	17	18	**19**	20	21	22
23	24	25	26	27	28	29
30						

July

S	M	T	W	T	F	S
	1	2	3	**4**	5	6
7	8	9	10	11	12	13
14	15	16	17	18	19	20
21	22	23	24	25	26	27
28	29	30	31			

August

S	M	T	W	T	F	S
				1	2	3
4	5	6	7	8	9	10
11	12	13	14	15	16	17
18	19	20	21	22	23	24
25	26	27	28	29	30	31

September

S	M	T	W	T	F	S
1	**2**	3	4	5	6	7
8	9	10	11	12	13	14
15	16	17	18	19	20	21
22	23	24	25	26	27	28
29	30					

October

S	M	T	W	T	F	S
		1	2	3	4	5
6	7	8	9	10	11	12
13	**14**	15	16	17	18	19
20	21	22	23	24	25	26
27	28	29	30	**31**		

November

S	M	T	W	T	F	S
					1	2
3	4	**5**	6	7	8	9
10	**11**	12	13	14	15	16
17	18	19	20	21	22	23
24	25	26	27	**28**	**29**	30

December

S	M	T	W	T	F	S
1	2	3	4	5	6	7
8	9	10	11	12	13	14
15	16	17	18	19	20	21
22	23	**24**	**25**	26	27	28
29	30	**31**				

Jan 1: New Year's Day
Jan 15: Martin Luther King Jr. Day
Feb 14: Valentine's Day
Feb 19: Washington's Birthday
Mar 17: St. Patrick's Day
Mar 31: Easter Sunday
Apr 15: Tax Day
Apr 24: Administrative Professionals Day

May 12: Mother's Day
May 27: Memorial Day
Jun 16: Father's Day
Jun 19: Juneteenth
Jul 4: Independence Day
Sep 2: Labor Day
Oct 14: Columbus Day
Oct 31: Halloween

Nov 5: Election Day
Nov 11: Veterans Day
Nov 28: Thanksgiving Day
Nov 29: Day after Thanksgiving Day
Dec 24: Christmas Eve
Dec 25: Christmas Day
Dec 31: New Year's Eve

2025

January

S	M	T	W	T	F	S
			1	2	3	4
5	6	7	8	9	10	11
12	13	14	15	16	17	18
19	**20**	21	22	23	24	25
26	27	28	29	30	31	

February

S	M	T	W	T	F	S
						1
2	3	4	5	6	7	8
9	10	11	12	13	**14**	15
16	**17**	18	19	20	21	22
23	24	25	26	27	28	

March

S	M	T	W	T	F	S
						1
2	3	4	5	6	7	8
9	10	11	12	13	14	15
16	**17**	18	19	20	21	22
23	24	25	26	27	28	29
30	31					

April

S	M	T	W	T	F	S
		1	2	3	4	5
6	7	8	9	10	11	12
13	14	**15**	16	17	18	19
20	21	22	**23**	24	25	26
27	28	29	30			

May

S	M	T	W	T	F	S
				1	2	3
4	5	6	7	8	9	10
11	12	13	14	15	16	17
18	19	20	21	22	23	24
25	**26**	27	28	29	30	31

June

S	M	T	W	T	F	S
1	2	3	4	5	6	7
8	9	10	11	12	13	14
15	16	17	18	**19**	20	21
22	23	24	25	26	27	28
29	30					

July

S	M	T	W	T	F	S
		1	2	3	**4**	5
6	7	8	9	10	11	12
13	14	15	16	17	18	19
20	21	22	23	24	25	26
27	28	29	30	31		

August

S	M	T	W	T	F	S
					1	2
3	4	5	6	7	8	9
10	11	12	13	14	15	16
17	18	19	20	21	22	23
24	25	26	27	28	29	30
31						

September

S	M	T	W	T	F	S
	1	2	3	4	5	6
7	8	9	10	11	12	13
14	15	16	17	18	19	20
21	22	23	24	25	26	27
28	29	30				

October

S	M	T	W	T	F	S
			1	2	3	4
5	6	7	8	9	10	11
12	**13**	14	15	16	17	18
19	20	21	22	23	24	25
26	27	28	29	30	**31**	

November

S	M	T	W	T	F	S
						1
2	3	4	5	6	7	8
9	10	**11**	12	13	14	15
16	17	18	19	20	21	22
23	24	25	26	**27**	**28**	29
30						

December

S	M	T	W	T	F	S
	1	2	3	4	5	6
7	8	9	10	11	12	13
14	15	16	17	18	19	20
21	22	23	**24**	**25**	26	27
28	29	30	**31**			

Jan 1: New Year's Day
Jan 20: Martin Luther King Jr. Day
Feb 14: Valentine's Day
Feb 17: Washington's Birthday
Mar 17: St. Patrick's Day
Apr 15: Tax Day
Apr 20: Easter Sunday
Apr 23: Administrative Professionals Day

May 11: Mother's Day
May 26: Memorial Day
Jun 15: Father's Day
Jun 19: Juneteenth
Jul 4: Independence Day
Sep 1: Labor Day
Oct 13: Columbus Day
Oct 31: Halloween

Nov 11: Veterans Day
Nov 27: Thanksgiving Day
Nov 28: Day after Thanksgiving Day
Dec 24: Christmas Eve
Dec 25: Christmas Day
Dec 31: New Year's Eve

2026

January

S	M	T	W	T	F	S
				1	2	3
4	5	6	7	8	9	10
11	12	13	14	15	16	17
18	**19**	20	21	22	23	24
25	26	27	28	29	30	31

February

S	M	T	W	T	F	S
1	2	3	4	5	6	7
8	9	10	11	12	13	**14**
15	**16**	17	18	19	20	21
22	23	24	25	26	27	28

March

S	M	T	W	T	F	S
1	2	3	4	5	6	7
8	9	10	11	12	13	14
15	16	**17**	18	19	20	21
22	23	24	25	26	27	28
29	30	31				

April

S	M	T	W	T	F	S
			1	2	3	4
5	6	7	8	9	10	11
12	13	14	**15**	16	17	18
19	20	21	**22**	23	24	25
26	27	28	29	30		

May

S	M	T	W	T	F	S
					1	2
3	4	5	6	7	8	9
10	11	12	13	14	15	16
17	18	19	20	21	22	23
24	**25**	26	27	28	29	30
31						

June

S	M	T	W	T	F	S
	1	2	3	4	5	6
7	8	9	10	11	12	13
14	15	16	17	18	**19**	20
21	22	23	24	25	26	27
28	29	30				

July

S	M	T	W	T	F	S
			1	2	**3**	**4**
5	6	7	8	9	10	11
12	13	14	15	16	17	18
19	20	21	22	23	24	25
26	27	28	29	30	31	

August

S	M	T	W	T	F	S
						1
2	3	4	5	6	7	8
9	10	11	12	13	14	15
16	17	18	19	20	21	22
23	24	25	26	27	28	29
30	31					

September

S	M	T	W	T	F	S
		1	2	3	4	5
6	**7**	8	9	10	11	12
13	14	15	16	17	18	19
20	21	22	23	24	25	26
27	28	29	30			

October

S	M	T	W	T	F	S
				1	2	3
4	5	6	7	8	9	10
11	**12**	13	14	15	16	17
18	19	20	21	22	23	24
25	26	27	28	29	30	**31**

November

S	M	T	W	T	F	S
1	2	3	4	5	6	7
8	9	10	**11**	12	13	14
15	16	17	18	19	20	21
22	23	24	25	**26**	**27**	28
29	30					

December

S	M	T	W	T	F	S
		1	2	3	4	5
6	7	8	9	10	11	12
13	14	15	16	17	18	19
20	21	22	23	**24**	**25**	26
27	28	29	30	**31**		

Jan 1: New Year's Day
Jan 19: Martin Luther King Jr. Day
Feb 14: Valentine's Day
Feb 16: Washington's Birthday
Mar 17: St. Patrick's Day
Apr 5: Easter Sunday
Apr 15: Tax Day
Apr 22: Administrative Professionals Day
May 10: Mother's Day
May 25: Memorial Day
Jun 19: Juneteenth
Jun 21: Father's Day
Jul 3: Independence Day (substitute day)
Jul 4: Independence Day
Sep 7: Labor Day
Oct 12: Columbus Day
Oct 31: Halloween
Nov 11: Veterans Day
Nov 26: Thanksgiving Day
Nov 27: Day after Thanksgiving Day
Dec 24: Christmas Eve
Dec 25: Christmas Day
Dec 31: New Year's Eve

Annual Notes

Projects List

Project Name:

Date Started: __________
Projected Word Count: __________

Date Finished: __________
Finished Word count: __________

Fiction/ Non Fiction Genre: __________

About:

Project Name:

Date Started: __________
Projected Word Count: __________

Date Finished: __________
Finished Word count: __________

Fiction/ Non Fiction Genre: __________

About:

Project Name:

Date Started: __________
Projected Word Count: __________

Date Finished: __________
Finished Word count: __________

Fiction/ Non Fiction Genre: __________

About:

Project Name:

Date Started: __________
Projected Word Count: __________

Date Finished: __________
Finished Word count: __________

Fiction/ Non Fiction Genre: __________

About:

Annual To-Do

JANUARY	FEBRUARY
MARCH	APRIL
MAY	JUNE
JULY	AUGUST
SEPTEMBER	OCTOBER
NOVEMBER	DECEMBER

TBR List

	BOOK TITLE	AUTHOR
☐		
☐		
☐		
☐		
☐		
☐		
☐		
☐		
☐		
☐		
☐		
☐		
☐		
☐		
☐		
☐		
☐		
☐		
☐		
☐		
☐		
☐		
☐		
☐		
☐		
☐		
☐		
☐		
☐		
☐		
☐		
☐		
☐		
☐		

Completed Reads

	BOOK TITLE	AUTHOR	DATE FINISHED
1			
2			
3			
4			
5			
6			
7			
8			
9			
10			
11			
12			
13			
14			
15			
16			
17			
18			
19			
20			
21			
22			
23			
24			
25			
26			
27			
28			
29			
30			

Month

Habit Tracker

	Write	Edit	Read	Post on Social Media	Scroll Through Media Feeds	Take Social Media Break	Marketing	Blog	Connected with Other Writers	Exercise	Get Outside	Self-care	Meditate							
1																				
2																				
3																				
4																				
5																				
6																				
7																				
8																				
9																				
10																				
11																				
12																				
13																				
14																				
15																				
16																				
17																				
18																				
19																				
20																				
21																				
22																				
23																				
24																				
25																				
26																				
27																				
28																				
29																				
30																				
31																				

Monthly Calendar

MONTH YEAR

SUNDAY	MONDAY	TUESDAY	WEDNESDAY	THURSDAY	FRIDAY	SATURDAY

To-Do List

MONTH: ______________________________

ITEMS CARRIED OVER FROM PREVIOUS MONTH

- [ ] ______________________ - [ ] ______________________
- [ ] ______________________ - [ ] ______________________
- [ ] ______________________ - [ ] ______________________

TOP PRIORITY

- [ ] ______________________ - [ ] ______________________
- [ ] ______________________ - [ ] ______________________
- [ ] ______________________ - [ ] ______________________
- [ ] ______________________ - [ ] ______________________

IMPORTANT

- [ ] ______________________ - [ ] ______________________
- [ ] ______________________ - [ ] ______________________
- [ ] ______________________ - [ ] ______________________
- [ ] ______________________ - [ ] ______________________

TO DO

- [ ] ______________________ - [ ] ______________________
- [ ] ______________________ - [ ] ______________________
- [ ] ______________________ - [ ] ______________________
- [ ] ______________________ - [ ] ______________________
- [ ] ______________________ - [ ] ______________________
- [ ] ______________________ - [ ] ______________________
- [ ] ______________________ - [ ] ______________________
- [ ] ______________________ - [ ] ______________________
- [ ] ______________________ - [ ] ______________________
- [ ] ______________________ - [ ] ______________________
- [ ] ______________________ - [ ] ______________________
- [ ] ______________________ - [ ] ______________________

Month's Notes

Almost all good writing
begins with
TERRIBLE
first efforts
You need to start somewhere

Month's Blog Posts

1

2

3

4

5

Weekly Calendar

WEEK MONTH YEAR

Cipher

writing time | editing time | social media | administration

	SUNDAY	MONDAY	TUESDAY	WEDNESDAY	THURSDAY	FRIDAY	SATURDAY
Date							
7:00 – 8:00							
8:00 – 9:00							
9:00 – 10:00							
10:00 – 11:00							
11:00 – 12:00							
12:00 – 1:00							
1:00 – 2:00							
2:00 – 3:00							
3:00 – 4:00							
4:00 – 5:00							
5:00 – 6:00							
6:00 – 7:00							
7:00 – 8:00							
8:00 – 9:00							
9:00 – 10:00							
10:00 – 11:00							

Weekly Social Media Posts

MONDAY	PLATFORM: POSTS 1. 2. NOTES:	PLATFORM: POSTS 1. 2. NOTES:	PLATFORM: POSTS 1. 2. NOTES:
TUESDAY	PLATFORM: POSTS 1. 2. NOTES:	PLATFORM: POSTS 1. 2. NOTES:	PLATFORM: POSTS 1. 2. NOTES:
WEDNESDAY	PLATFORM: POSTS 1. 2. NOTES:	PLATFORM: POSTS 1. 2. NOTES:	PLATFORM: POSTS 1. 2. NOTES:
THURSDAY	PLATFORM: POSTS 1. 2. NOTES:	PLATFORM: POSTS 1. 2. NOTES:	PLATFORM: POSTS 1. 2. NOTES:
FRIDAY	PLATFORM: POSTS 1. 2. NOTES:	PLATFORM: POSTS 1. 2. NOTES:	PLATFORM: POSTS 1. 2. NOTES:

WEEKEND	SATURDAY	SUNDAY
	POSTS (PLATFORM) 1. 2. NOTES:	POSTS (PLATFORM) 1. 2. NOTES:

Weekly Journal / Writing Notes

freestyle
(yourstyle)
Love
BROKEN

Weekly Calendar

WEEK MONTH YEAR

Cipher

writing time	editing time	social media	administration			

	SUNDAY	MONDAY	TUESDAY	WEDNESDAY	THURSDAY	FRIDAY	SATURDAY
Date							
7:00 – 8:00							
8:00 – 9:00							
9:00 – 10:00							
10:00 – 11:00							
11:00 – 12:00							
12:00 – 1:00							
1:00 – 2:00							
2:00 – 3:00							
3:00 – 4:00							
4:00 – 5:00							
5:00 – 6:00							
6:00 – 7:00							
7:00 – 8:00							
8:00 – 9:00							
9:00 – 10:00							
10:00 – 11:00							

Weekly Social Media Posts

MONDAY	PLATFORM: POSTS 1. 2. NOTES:	PLATFORM: POSTS 1. 2. NOTES:	PLATFORM: POSTS 1. 2. NOTES:
TUESDAY	PLATFORM: POSTS 1. 2. NOTES:	PLATFORM: POSTS 1. 2. NOTES:	PLATFORM: POSTS 1. 2. NOTES:
WEDNESDAY	PLATFORM: POSTS 1. 2. NOTES:	PLATFORM: POSTS 1. 2. NOTES:	PLATFORM: POSTS 1. 2. NOTES:
THURSDAY	PLATFORM: POSTS 1. 2. NOTES:	PLATFORM: POSTS 1. 2. NOTES:	PLATFORM: POSTS 1. 2. NOTES:
FRIDAY	PLATFORM: POSTS 1. 2. NOTES:	PLATFORM: POSTS 1. 2. NOTES:	PLATFORM: POSTS 1. 2. NOTES:

WEEKEND	SATURDAY	SUNDAY
	POSTS (PLATFORM) 1. 2. NOTES:	POSTS (PLATFORM) 1. 2. NOTES:

Weekly Journal / Writing Notes

freestyle
(yourstyle)

Weekly Calendar

WEEK MONTH YEAR

Cipher: writing time | editing time | social media | administration

	SUNDAY	MONDAY	TUESDAY	WEDNESDAY	THURSDAY	FRIDAY	SATURDAY
Date							
7:00 – 8:00							
8:00 – 9:00							
9:00 – 10:00							
10:00 – 11:00							
11:00 – 12:00							
12:00 – 1:00							
1:00 – 2:00							
2:00 – 3:00							
3:00 – 4:00							
4:00 – 5:00							
5:00 – 6:00							
6:00 – 7:00							
7:00 – 8:00							
8:00 – 9:00							
9:00 – 10:00							
10:00 – 11:00							

Weekly Social Media Posts

MONDAY	PLATFORM: POSTS 1. 2. NOTES:	PLATFORM: POSTS 1. 2. NOTES:	PLATFORM: POSTS 1. 2. NOTES:
TUESDAY	PLATFORM: POSTS 1. 2. NOTES:	PLATFORM: POSTS 1. 2. NOTES:	PLATFORM: POSTS 1. 2. NOTES:
WEDNESDAY	PLATFORM: POSTS 1. 2. NOTES:	PLATFORM: POSTS 1. 2. NOTES:	PLATFORM: POSTS 1. 2. NOTES:
THURSDAY	PLATFORM: POSTS 1. 2. NOTES:	PLATFORM: POSTS 1. 2. NOTES:	PLATFORM: POSTS 1. 2. NOTES:
FRIDAY	PLATFORM: POSTS 1. 2. NOTES:	PLATFORM: POSTS 1. 2. NOTES:	PLATFORM: POSTS 1. 2. NOTES:

WEEKEND	SATURDAY POSTS (PLATFORM) 1. 2. NOTES:	SUNDAY POSTS (PLATFORM) 1. 2. NOTES:

Weekly Journal / Writing Notes

freestyle
(yourstyle)

Weekly Calendar

WEEK MONTH YEAR

Cipher

writing time	editing time	social media	administration			

	SUNDAY	MONDAY	TUESDAY	WEDNESDAY	THURSDAY	FRIDAY	SATURDAY
Date							
7:00 – 8:00							
8:00 – 9:00							
9:00 – 10:00							
10:00 – 11:00							
11:00 – 12:00							
12:00 – 1:00							
1:00 – 2:00							
2:00 – 3:00							
3:00 – 4:00							
4:00 – 5:00							
5:00 – 6:00							
6:00 – 7:00							
7:00 – 8:00							
8:00 – 9:00							
9:00 – 10:00							
10:00 – 11:00							

Weekly Social Media Posts

MONDAY	PLATFORM: POSTS 1. 2. NOTES:	PLATFORM: POSTS 1. 2. NOTES:	PLATFORM: POSTS 1. 2. NOTES:
TUESDAY	PLATFORM: POSTS 1. 2. NOTES:	PLATFORM: POSTS 1. 2. NOTES:	PLATFORM: POSTS 1. 2. NOTES:
WEDNESDAY	PLATFORM: POSTS 1. 2. NOTES:	PLATFORM: POSTS 1. 2. NOTES:	PLATFORM: POSTS 1. 2. NOTES:
THURSDAY	PLATFORM: POSTS 1. 2. NOTES:	PLATFORM: POSTS 1. 2. NOTES:	PLATFORM: POSTS 1. 2. NOTES:
FRIDAY	PLATFORM: POSTS 1. 2. NOTES:	PLATFORM: POSTS 1. 2. NOTES:	PLATFORM: POSTS 1. 2. NOTES:

WEEKEND	SATURDAY	SUNDAY
	POSTS (PLATFORM) 1. 2. NOTES:	POSTS (PLATFORM) 1. 2. NOTES:

Weekly Journal / Writing Notes

freestyle
(yourstyle)

Weekly Calendar

WEEK MONTH YEAR

Cipher: writing time | editing time | social media | administration

Date	SUNDAY	MONDAY	TUESDAY	WEDNESDAY	THURSDAY	FRIDAY	SATURDAY
7:00 – 8:00							
8:00 – 9:00							
9:00 – 10:00							
10:00 – 11:00							
11:00 – 12:00							
12:00 – 1:00							
1:00 – 2:00							
2:00 – 3:00							
3:00 – 4:00							
4:00 – 5:00							
5:00 – 6:00							
6:00 – 7:00							
7:00 – 8:00							
8:00 – 9:00							
9:00 – 10:00							
10:00 – 11:00							

Weekly Social Media Posts

MONDAY	PLATFORM: POSTS 1. 2. NOTES:	PLATFORM: POSTS 1. 2. NOTES:	PLATFORM: POSTS 1. 2. NOTES:
TUESDAY	PLATFORM: POSTS 1. 2. NOTES:	PLATFORM: POSTS 1. 2. NOTES:	PLATFORM: POSTS 1. 2. NOTES:
WEDNESDAY	PLATFORM: POSTS 1. 2. NOTES:	PLATFORM: POSTS 1. 2. NOTES:	PLATFORM: POSTS 1. 2. NOTES:
THURSDAY	PLATFORM: POSTS 1. 2. NOTES:	PLATFORM: POSTS 1. 2. NOTES:	PLATFORM: POSTS 1. 2. NOTES:
FRIDAY	PLATFORM: POSTS 1. 2. NOTES:	PLATFORM: POSTS 1. 2. NOTES:	PLATFORM: POSTS 1. 2. NOTES:

WEEKEND	SATURDAY	SUNDAY
	POSTS (PLATFORM) 1. 2. NOTES:	POSTS (PLATFORM) 1. 2. NOTES:

Weekly Journal / Writing Notes

freestyle
(yourstyle)

Month

Habit Tracker

	Write	Edit	Read	Post on Social Media	Scroll Through Media Feeds	Take Social Media Break	Marketing	Blog	Connected with Other Writers	Exercise	Get Outside	Self-care	Meditate							
1																				
2																				
3																				
4																				
5																				
6																				
7																				
8																				
9																				
10																				
11																				
12																				
13																				
14																				
15																				
16																				
17																				
18																				
19																				
20																				
21																				
22																				
23																				
24																				
25																				
26																				
27																				
28																				
29																				
30																				
31																				

Monthly Calendar

MONTH YEAR

SUNDAY	MONDAY	TUESDAY	WEDNESDAY	THURSDAY	FRIDAY	SATURDAY

To-Do List

MONTH: ____________________

ITEMS CARRIED OVER FROM PREVIOUS MONTH

- [ ] ____________________ - [ ] ____________________
- [ ] ____________________ - [ ] ____________________
- [ ] ____________________ - [ ] ____________________

TOP PRIORITY

- [ ] ____________________ - [ ] ____________________
- [ ] ____________________ - [ ] ____________________
- [ ] ____________________ - [ ] ____________________
- [ ] ____________________ - [ ] ____________________

IMPORTANT

- [ ] ____________________ - [ ] ____________________
- [ ] ____________________ - [ ] ____________________
- [ ] ____________________ - [ ] ____________________
- [ ] ____________________ - [ ] ____________________

TO DO

- [ ] ____________________ - [ ] ____________________
- [ ] ____________________ - [ ] ____________________
- [ ] ____________________ - [ ] ____________________
- [ ] ____________________ - [ ] ____________________
- [ ] ____________________ - [ ] ____________________
- [ ] ____________________ - [ ] ____________________
- [ ] ____________________ - [ ] ____________________
- [ ] ____________________ - [ ] ____________________
- [ ] ____________________ - [ ] ____________________
- [ ] ____________________ - [ ] ____________________
- [ ] ____________________ - [ ] ____________________
- [ ] ____________________ - [ ] ____________________

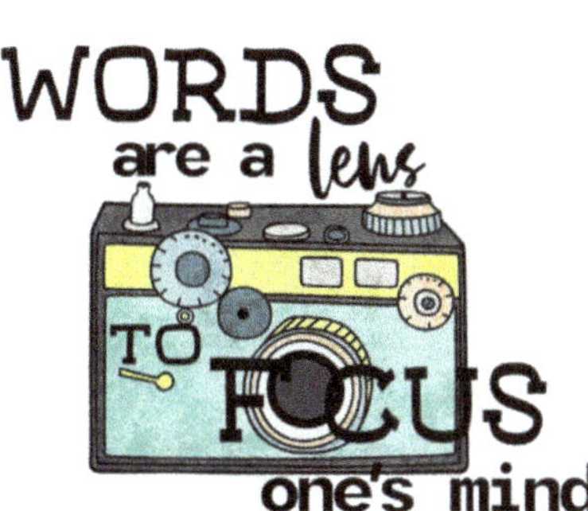

Month's Notes

Month's Blog Posts

1

2

3

4

5

Weekly Calendar

WEEK MONTH YEAR

Cipher: writing time | editing time | social media | administration

Date	SUNDAY	MONDAY	TUESDAY	WEDNESDAY	THURSDAY	FRIDAY	SATURDAY
7:00 – 8:00							
8:00 – 9:00							
9:00 – 10:00							
10:00 – 11:00							
11:00 – 12:00							
12:00 – 1:00							
1:00 – 2:00							
2:00 – 3:00							
3:00 – 4:00							
4:00 – 5:00							
5:00 – 6:00							
6:00 – 7:00							
7:00 – 8:00							
8:00 – 9:00							
9:00 – 10:00							
10:00 – 11:00							

Weekly Social Media Posts

MONDAY	PLATFORM: POSTS 1. 2. NOTES:	PLATFORM: POSTS 1. 2. NOTES:	PLATFORM: POSTS 1. 2. NOTES:
TUESDAY	PLATFORM: POSTS 1. 2. NOTES:	PLATFORM: POSTS 1. 2. NOTES:	PLATFORM: POSTS 1. 2. NOTES:
WEDNESDAY	PLATFORM: POSTS 1. 2. NOTES:	PLATFORM: POSTS 1. 2. NOTES:	PLATFORM: POSTS 1. 2. NOTES:
THURSDAY	PLATFORM: POSTS 1. 2. NOTES:	PLATFORM: POSTS 1. 2. NOTES:	PLATFORM: POSTS 1. 2. NOTES:
FRIDAY	PLATFORM: POSTS 1. 2. NOTES:	PLATFORM: POSTS 1. 2. NOTES:	PLATFORM: POSTS 1. 2. NOTES:

WEEKEND	SATURDAY	SUNDAY
	POSTS (PLATFORM) 1. 2. NOTES:	POSTS (PLATFORM) 1. 2. NOTES:

Weekly Journal / Writing Notes

freestyle
(yourstyle)
LOVE
BROKEN

Weekly Calendar

WEEK MONTH YEAR

Cipher: writing time | editing time | social media | administration

	SUNDAY	MONDAY	TUESDAY	WEDNESDAY	THURSDAY	FRIDAY	SATURDAY
Date							
7:00 – 8:00							
8:00 – 9:00							
9:00 – 10:00							
10:00 – 11:00							
11:00 – 12:00							
12:00 – 1:00							
1:00 – 2:00							
2:00 – 3:00							
3:00 – 4:00							
4:00 – 5:00							
5:00 – 6:00							
6:00 – 7:00							
7:00 – 8:00							
8:00 – 9:00							
9:00 – 10:00							
10:00 – 11:00							

Weekly Social Media Posts

MONDAY	PLATFORM: POSTS 1. 2. NOTES:	PLATFORM: POSTS 1. 2. NOTES:	PLATFORM: POSTS 1. 2. NOTES:
TUESDAY	PLATFORM: POSTS 1. 2. NOTES:	PLATFORM: POSTS 1. 2. NOTES:	PLATFORM: POSTS 1. 2. NOTES:
WEDNESDAY	PLATFORM: POSTS 1. 2. NOTES:	PLATFORM: POSTS 1. 2. NOTES:	PLATFORM: POSTS 1. 2. NOTES:
THURSDAY	PLATFORM: POSTS 1. 2. NOTES:	PLATFORM: POSTS 1. 2. NOTES:	PLATFORM: POSTS 1. 2. NOTES:
FRIDAY	PLATFORM: POSTS 1. 2. NOTES:	PLATFORM: POSTS 1. 2. NOTES:	PLATFORM: POSTS 1. 2. NOTES:

WEEKEND	SATURDAY	SUNDAY
	POSTS (PLATFORM) 1. 2. NOTES:	POSTS (PLATFORM) 1. 2. NOTES:

Weekly Journal / Writing Notes

freestyle
(yourstyle)

Weekly Calendar

WEEK MONTH YEAR

Cipher: writing time | editing time | social media | administration | ___ | ___ | ___

	SUNDAY	MONDAY	TUESDAY	WEDNESDAY	THURSDAY	FRIDAY	SATURDAY
Date							
7:00 – 8:00							
8:00 – 9:00							
9:00 – 10:00							
10:00 – 11:00							
11:00 – 12:00							
12:00 – 1:00							
1:00 – 2:00							
2:00 – 3:00							
3:00 – 4:00							
4:00 – 5:00							
5:00 – 6:00							
6:00 – 7:00							
7:00 – 8:00							
8:00 – 9:00							
9:00 – 10:00							
10:00 – 11:00							

Weekly Social Media Posts

MONDAY	PLATFORM: POSTS 1. 2. NOTES:	PLATFORM: POSTS 1. 2. NOTES:	PLATFORM: POSTS 1. 2. NOTES:
TUESDAY	PLATFORM: POSTS 1. 2. NOTES:	PLATFORM: POSTS 1. 2. NOTES:	PLATFORM: POSTS 1. 2. NOTES:
WEDNESDAY	PLATFORM: POSTS 1. 2. NOTES:	PLATFORM: POSTS 1. 2. NOTES:	PLATFORM: POSTS 1. 2. NOTES:
THURSDAY	PLATFORM: POSTS 1. 2. NOTES:	PLATFORM: POSTS 1. 2. NOTES:	PLATFORM: POSTS 1. 2. NOTES:
FRIDAY	PLATFORM: POSTS 1. 2. NOTES:	PLATFORM: POSTS 1. 2. NOTES:	PLATFORM: POSTS 1. 2. NOTES:

WEEKEND	SATURDAY	SUNDAY
	POSTS (PLATFORM) 1. 2. NOTES:	POSTS (PLATFORM) 1. 2. NOTES:

Weekly Journal / Writing Notes

freestyle
(yourstyle)

Weekly Calendar

WEEK MONTH YEAR

Cipher: writing time, editing time, social media, administration

	SUNDAY	MONDAY	TUESDAY	WEDNESDAY	THURSDAY	FRIDAY	SATURDAY
Date							
7:00 – 8:00							
8:00 – 9:00							
9:00 – 10:00							
10:00 – 11:00							
11:00 – 12:00							
12:00 – 1:00							
1:00 – 2:00							
2:00 – 3:00							
3:00 – 4:00							
4:00 – 5:00							
5:00 – 6:00							
6:00 – 7:00							
7:00 – 8:00							
8:00 – 9:00							
9:00 – 10:00							
10:00 – 11:00							

Weekly Social Media Posts

MONDAY	PLATFORM: POSTS 1. 2. NOTES:	PLATFORM: POSTS 1. 2. NOTES:	PLATFORM: POSTS 1. 2. NOTES:
TUESDAY	PLATFORM: POSTS 1. 2. NOTES:	PLATFORM: POSTS 1. 2. NOTES:	PLATFORM: POSTS 1. 2. NOTES:
WEDNESDAY	PLATFORM: POSTS 1. 2. NOTES:	PLATFORM: POSTS 1. 2. NOTES:	PLATFORM: POSTS 1. 2. NOTES:
THURSDAY	PLATFORM: POSTS 1. 2. NOTES:	PLATFORM: POSTS 1. 2. NOTES:	PLATFORM: POSTS 1. 2. NOTES:
FRIDAY	PLATFORM: POSTS 1. 2. NOTES:	PLATFORM: POSTS 1. 2. NOTES:	PLATFORM: POSTS 1. 2. NOTES:

WEEKEND	SATURDAY	SUNDAY
	POSTS (PLATFORM) 1. 2. NOTES:	POSTS (PLATFORM) 1. 2. NOTES:

Weekly Journal / Writing Notes

freestyle
(yourstyle)

Weekly Calendar

WEEK MONTH YEAR

Cipher: writing time | editing time | social media | administration | ___ | ___ | ___

	SUNDAY	MONDAY	TUESDAY	WEDNESDAY	THURSDAY	FRIDAY	SATURDAY
Date							
7:00 – 8:00							
8:00 – 9:00							
9:00 – 10:00							
10:00 – 11:00							
11:00 – 12:00							
12:00 – 1:00							
1:00 – 2:00							
2:00 – 3:00							
3:00 – 4:00							
4:00 – 5:00							
5:00 – 6:00							
6:00 – 7:00							
7:00 – 8:00							
8:00 – 9:00							
9:00 – 10:00							
10:00 – 11:00							

Weekly Social Media Posts

MONDAY	PLATFORM: POSTS 1. 2. NOTES:	PLATFORM: POSTS 1. 2. NOTES:	PLATFORM: POSTS 1. 2. NOTES:
TUESDAY	PLATFORM: POSTS 1. 2. NOTES:	PLATFORM: POSTS 1. 2. NOTES:	PLATFORM: POSTS 1. 2. NOTES:
WEDNESDAY	PLATFORM: POSTS 1. 2. NOTES:	PLATFORM: POSTS 1. 2. NOTES:	PLATFORM: POSTS 1. 2. NOTES:
THURSDAY	PLATFORM: POSTS 1. 2. NOTES:	PLATFORM: POSTS 1. 2. NOTES:	PLATFORM: POSTS 1. 2. NOTES:
FRIDAY	PLATFORM: POSTS 1. 2. NOTES:	PLATFORM: POSTS 1. 2. NOTES:	PLATFORM: POSTS 1. 2. NOTES:

WEEKEND	SATURDAY	SUNDAY
	POSTS (PLATFORM) 1. 2. NOTES:	POSTS (PLATFORM) 1. 2. NOTES:

Weekly Journal / Writing Notes

freestyle
(yourstyle)

Month

Habit Tracker

	Write	Edit	Read	Post on Social Media	Scroll Through Media Feeds	Take Social Media Break	Marketing	Blog	Connected with Other Writers	Exercise	Get Outside	Self-care	Meditate							
1																				
2																				
3																				
4																				
5																				
6																				
7																				
8																				
9																				
10																				
11																				
12																				
13																				
14																				
15																				
16																				
17																				
18																				
19																				
20																				
21																				
22																				
23																				
24																				
25																				
26																				
27																				
28																				
29																				
30																				
31																				

Monthly Calendar

MONTH YEAR

SUNDAY	MONDAY	TUESDAY	WEDNESDAY	THURSDAY	FRIDAY	SATURDAY

To-Do List

MONTH: ______________________

ITEMS CARRIED OVER FROM PREVIOUS MONTH

- [ ] ______________ - [ ] ______________
- [ ] ______________ - [ ] ______________
- [ ] ______________ - [ ] ______________

TOP PRIORITY

- [ ] ______________ - [ ] ______________
- [ ] ______________ - [ ] ______________
- [ ] ______________ - [ ] ______________
- [ ] ______________ - [ ] ______________

IMPORTANT

- [ ] ______________ - [ ] ______________
- [ ] ______________ - [ ] ______________
- [ ] ______________ - [ ] ______________
- [ ] ______________ - [ ] ______________

TO DO

- [ ] ______________ - [ ] ______________
- [ ] ______________ - [ ] ______________
- [ ] ______________ - [ ] ______________
- [ ] ______________ - [ ] ______________
- [ ] ______________ - [ ] ______________
- [ ] ______________ - [ ] ______________
- [ ] ______________ - [ ] ______________
- [ ] ______________ - [ ] ______________
- [ ] ______________ - [ ] ______________
- [ ] ______________ - [ ] ______________
- [ ] ______________ - [ ] ______________
- [ ] ______________ - [ ] ______________

Month's Notes

You can make anything by writing

Month's Blog Posts

1

2

3

4

5

Weekly Calendar

WEEK MONTH YEAR

Cipher

writing time | editing time | social media | administration

	SUNDAY	MONDAY	TUESDAY	WEDNESDAY	THURSDAY	FRIDAY	SATURDAY
Date							
7:00 – 8:00							
8:00 – 9:00							
9:00 – 10:00							
10:00 – 11:00							
11:00 – 12:00							
12:00 – 1:00							
1:00 – 2:00							
2:00 – 3:00							
3:00 – 4:00							
4:00 – 5:00							
5:00 – 6:00							
6:00 – 7:00							
7:00 – 8:00							
8:00 – 9:00							
9:00 – 10:00							
10:00 – 11:00							

Weekly Social Media Posts

MONDAY	PLATFORM: POSTS 1. 2. NOTES:	PLATFORM: POSTS 1. 2. NOTES:	PLATFORM: POSTS 1. 2. NOTES:
TUESDAY	PLATFORM: POSTS 1. 2. NOTES:	PLATFORM: POSTS 1. 2. NOTES:	PLATFORM: POSTS 1. 2. NOTES:
WEDNESDAY	PLATFORM: POSTS 1. 2. NOTES:	PLATFORM: POSTS 1. 2. NOTES:	PLATFORM: POSTS 1. 2. NOTES:
THURSDAY	PLATFORM: POSTS 1. 2. NOTES:	PLATFORM: POSTS 1. 2. NOTES:	PLATFORM: POSTS 1. 2. NOTES:
FRIDAY	PLATFORM: POSTS 1. 2. NOTES:	PLATFORM: POSTS 1. 2. NOTES:	PLATFORM: POSTS 1. 2. NOTES:

WEEKEND	SATURDAY	SUNDAY
	POSTS (PLATFORM) 1. 2. NOTES:	POSTS (PLATFORM) 1. 2. NOTES:

Weekly Journal / Writing Notes

freestyle
(yourstyle)
LOVE
BROKEN

Weekly Calendar

WEEK MONTH YEAR

Cipher: writing time | editing time | social media | administration | ___ | ___ | ___

	SUNDAY	MONDAY	TUESDAY	WEDNESDAY	THURSDAY	FRIDAY	SATURDAY
Date							
7:00 – 8:00							
8:00 – 9:00							
9:00 – 10:00							
10:00 – 11:00							
11:00 – 12:00							
12:00 – 1:00							
1:00 – 2:00							
2:00 – 3:00							
3:00 – 4:00							
4:00 – 5:00							
5:00 – 6:00							
6:00 – 7:00							
7:00 – 8:00							
8:00 – 9:00							
9:00 – 10:00							
10:00 – 11:00							

Weekly Social Media Posts

MONDAY

PLATFORM:	PLATFORM:	PLATFORM:
POSTS	POSTS	POSTS
1.	1.	1.
2.	2.	2.
NOTES:	NOTES:	NOTES:

TUESDAY

PLATFORM:	PLATFORM:	PLATFORM:
POSTS	POSTS	POSTS
1.	1.	1.
2.	2.	2.
NOTES:	NOTES:	NOTES:

WEDNESDAY

PLATFORM:	PLATFORM:	PLATFORM:
POSTS	POSTS	POSTS
1.	1.	1.
2.	2.	2.
NOTES:	NOTES:	NOTES:

THURSDAY

PLATFORM:	PLATFORM:	PLATFORM:
POSTS	POSTS	POSTS
1.	1.	1.
2.	2.	2.
NOTES:	NOTES:	NOTES:

FRIDAY

PLATFORM:	PLATFORM:	PLATFORM:
POSTS	POSTS	POSTS
1.	1.	1.
2.	2.	2.
NOTES:	NOTES:	NOTES:

WEEKEND

SATURDAY	SUNDAY
POSTS (PLATFORM)	POSTS (PLATFORM)
1.	1.
2.	2.
NOTES:	NOTES:

Weekly Journal / Writing Notes

freestyle
(yourstyle)

Weekly Calendar

WEEK MONTH YEAR

Cipher: writing time | editing time | social media | administration

Date	SUNDAY	MONDAY	TUESDAY	WEDNESDAY	THURSDAY	FRIDAY	SATURDAY
7:00 – 8:00							
8:00 – 9:00							
9:00 – 10:00							
10:00 – 11:00							
11:00 – 12:00							
12:00 – 1:00							
1:00 – 2:00							
2:00 – 3:00							
3:00 – 4:00							
4:00 – 5:00							
5:00 – 6:00							
6:00 – 7:00							
7:00 – 8:00							
8:00 – 9:00							
9:00 – 10:00							
10:00 – 11:00							

Weekly Social Media Posts

MONDAY	PLATFORM: POSTS 1. 2. NOTES:	PLATFORM: POSTS 1. 2. NOTES:	PLATFORM: POSTS 1. 2. NOTES:
TUESDAY	PLATFORM: POSTS 1. 2. NOTES:	PLATFORM: POSTS 1. 2. NOTES:	PLATFORM: POSTS 1. 2. NOTES:
WEDNESDAY	PLATFORM: POSTS 1. 2. NOTES:	PLATFORM: POSTS 1. 2. NOTES:	PLATFORM: POSTS 1. 2. NOTES:
THURSDAY	PLATFORM: POSTS 1. 2. NOTES:	PLATFORM: POSTS 1. 2. NOTES:	PLATFORM: POSTS 1. 2. NOTES:
FRIDAY	PLATFORM: POSTS 1. 2. NOTES:	PLATFORM: POSTS 1. 2. NOTES:	PLATFORM: POSTS 1. 2. NOTES:

WEEKEND	SATURDAY	SUNDAY
	POSTS (PLATFORM) 1. 2. NOTES:	POSTS (PLATFORM) 1. 2. NOTES:

Weekly Journal / Writing Notes

freestyle
(yourstyle)

Weekly Calendar

WEEK MONTH YEAR

Cipher

writing time	editing time	social media	administration			

	SUNDAY	MONDAY	TUESDAY	WEDNESDAY	THURSDAY	FRIDAY	SATURDAY
Date							
7:00 – 8:00							
8:00 – 9:00							
9:00 – 10:00							
10:00 – 11:00							
11:00 – 12:00							
12:00 – 1:00							
1:00 – 2:00							
2:00 – 3:00							
3:00 – 4:00							
4:00 – 5:00							
5:00 – 6:00							
6:00 – 7:00							
7:00 – 8:00							
8:00 – 9:00							
9:00 – 10:00							
10:00 – 11:00							

Weekly Social Media Posts

MONDAY	PLATFORM: POSTS 1. 2. NOTES:	PLATFORM: POSTS 1. 2. NOTES:	PLATFORM: POSTS 1. 2. NOTES:
TUESDAY	PLATFORM: POSTS 1. 2. NOTES:	PLATFORM: POSTS 1. 2. NOTES:	PLATFORM: POSTS 1. 2. NOTES:
WEDNESDAY	PLATFORM: POSTS 1. 2. NOTES:	PLATFORM: POSTS 1. 2. NOTES:	PLATFORM: POSTS 1. 2. NOTES:
THURSDAY	PLATFORM: POSTS 1. 2. NOTES:	PLATFORM: POSTS 1. 2. NOTES:	PLATFORM: POSTS 1. 2. NOTES:
FRIDAY	PLATFORM: POSTS 1. 2. NOTES:	PLATFORM: POSTS 1. 2. NOTES:	PLATFORM: POSTS 1. 2. NOTES:

WEEKEND	SATURDAY	SUNDAY
	POSTS (PLATFORM) 1. 2. NOTES:	POSTS (PLATFORM) 1. 2. NOTES:

Weekly Journal / Writing Notes

freestyle
(yourstyle)

Weekly Calendar

WEEK MONTH YEAR

Cipher

writing time	editing time	social media	administration			

	SUNDAY	MONDAY	TUESDAY	WEDNESDAY	THURSDAY	FRIDAY	SATURDAY
Date							
7:00 – 8:00							
8:00 – 9:00							
9:00 – 10:00							
10:00 – 11:00							
11:00 – 12:00							
12:00 – 1:00							
1:00 – 2:00							
2:00 – 3:00							
3:00 – 4:00							
4:00 – 5:00							
5:00 – 6:00							
6:00 – 7:00							
7:00 – 8:00							
8:00 – 9:00							
9:00 – 10:00							
10:00 – 11:00							

Weekly Social Media Posts

MONDAY	PLATFORM: POSTS 1. 2. NOTES:	PLATFORM: POSTS 1. 2. NOTES:	PLATFORM: POSTS 1. 2. NOTES:
TUESDAY	PLATFORM: POSTS 1. 2. NOTES:	PLATFORM: POSTS 1. 2. NOTES:	PLATFORM: POSTS 1. 2. NOTES:
WEDNESDAY	PLATFORM: POSTS 1. 2. NOTES:	PLATFORM: POSTS 1. 2. NOTES:	PLATFORM: POSTS 1. 2. NOTES:
THURSDAY	PLATFORM: POSTS 1. 2. NOTES:	PLATFORM: POSTS 1. 2. NOTES:	PLATFORM: POSTS 1. 2. NOTES:
FRIDAY	PLATFORM: POSTS 1. 2. NOTES:	PLATFORM: POSTS 1. 2. NOTES:	PLATFORM: POSTS 1. 2. NOTES:

WEEKEND	SATURDAY	SUNDAY
	POSTS (PLATFORM) 1. 2. NOTES:	POSTS (PLATFORM) 1. 2. NOTES:

Weekly Journal / Writing Notes

freestyle
(yourstyle)

Month

Habit Tracker

	Write	Edit	Read	Post on Social Media	Scroll Through Media Feeds	Take Social Media Break	Marketing	Blog	Connected with Other Writers	Exercise	Get Outside	Self-care	Meditate							
1																				
2																				
3																				
4																				
5																				
6																				
7																				
8																				
9																				
10																				
11																				
12																				
13																				
14																				
15																				
16																				
17																				
18																				
19																				
20																				
21																				
22																				
23																				
24																				
25																				
26																				
27																				
28																				
29																				
30																				
31																				

Monthly Calendar

MONTH YEAR

SUNDAY	MONDAY	TUESDAY	WEDNESDAY	THURSDAY	FRIDAY	SATURDAY

To-Do List

MONTH: ____________________

ITEMS CARRIED OVER FROM PREVIOUS MONTH

- [ ] ____________________ - [ ] ____________________
- [ ] ____________________ - [ ] ____________________
- [ ] ____________________ - [ ] ____________________

TOP PRIORITY

- [ ] ____________________ - [ ] ____________________
- [ ] ____________________ - [ ] ____________________
- [ ] ____________________ - [ ] ____________________
- [ ] ____________________ - [ ] ____________________

IMPORTANT

- [ ] ____________________ - [ ] ____________________
- [ ] ____________________ - [ ] ____________________
- [ ] ____________________ - [ ] ____________________
- [ ] ____________________ - [ ] ____________________

TO DO

- [ ] ____________________ - [ ] ____________________
- [ ] ____________________ - [ ] ____________________
- [ ] ____________________ - [ ] ____________________
- [ ] ____________________ - [ ] ____________________
- [ ] ____________________ - [ ] ____________________
- [ ] ____________________ - [ ] ____________________
- [ ] ____________________ - [ ] ____________________
- [ ] ____________________ - [ ] ____________________
- [ ] ____________________ - [ ] ____________________
- [ ] ____________________ - [ ] ____________________
- [ ] ____________________ - [ ] ____________________
- [ ] ____________________ - [ ] ____________________

So the writer who breeds
more words than he needs
is making a chore
for the reader who reads

Month's Notes

Month's Blog Posts

1

2

3

4

5

Weekly Calendar

WEEK MONTH YEAR

Cipher

writing time	editing time	social media	administration			

	SUNDAY	MONDAY	TUESDAY	WEDNESDAY	THURSDAY	FRIDAY	SATURDAY
Date							
7:00 – 8:00							
8:00 – 9:00							
9:00 – 10:00							
10:00 – 11:00							
11:00 – 12:00							
12:00 – 1:00							
1:00 – 2:00							
2:00 – 3:00							
3:00 – 4:00							
4:00 – 5:00							
5:00 – 6:00							
6:00 – 7:00							
7:00 – 8:00							
8:00 – 9:00							
9:00 – 10:00							
10:00 – 11:00							

Weekly Social Media Posts

MONDAY	PLATFORM: POSTS 1. 2. NOTES:	PLATFORM: POSTS 1. 2. NOTES:	PLATFORM: POSTS 1. 2. NOTES:
TUESDAY	PLATFORM: POSTS 1. 2. NOTES:	PLATFORM: POSTS 1. 2. NOTES:	PLATFORM: POSTS 1. 2. NOTES:
WEDNESDAY	PLATFORM: POSTS 1. 2. NOTES:	PLATFORM: POSTS 1. 2. NOTES:	PLATFORM: POSTS 1. 2. NOTES:
THURSDAY	PLATFORM: POSTS 1. 2. NOTES:	PLATFORM: POSTS 1. 2. NOTES:	PLATFORM: POSTS 1. 2. NOTES:
FRIDAY	PLATFORM: POSTS 1. 2. NOTES:	PLATFORM: POSTS 1. 2. NOTES:	PLATFORM: POSTS 1. 2. NOTES:

WEEKEND	SATURDAY	SUNDAY
	POSTS (PLATFORM) 1. 2. NOTES:	POSTS (PLATFORM) 1. 2. NOTES:

Weekly Journal / Writing Notes

freestyle
(yourstyle)
LOVE
BROKEN

Weekly Calendar

WEEK MONTH YEAR

Cipher: writing time | editing time | social media | administration

	SUNDAY	MONDAY	TUESDAY	WEDNESDAY	THURSDAY	FRIDAY	SATURDAY
Date							
7:00 – 8:00							
8:00 – 9:00							
9:00 – 10:00							
10:00 – 11:00							
11:00 – 12:00							
12:00 – 1:00							
1:00 – 2:00							
2:00 – 3:00							
3:00 – 4:00							
4:00 – 5:00							
5:00 – 6:00							
6:00 – 7:00							
7:00 – 8:00							
8:00 – 9:00							
9:00 – 10:00							
10:00 – 11:00							

Weekly Social Media Posts

MONDAY	PLATFORM: POSTS 1. 2. NOTES:	PLATFORM: POSTS 1. 2. NOTES:	PLATFORM: POSTS 1. 2. NOTES:
TUESDAY	PLATFORM: POSTS 1. 2. NOTES:	PLATFORM: POSTS 1. 2. NOTES:	PLATFORM: POSTS 1. 2. NOTES:
WEDNESDAY	PLATFORM: POSTS 1. 2. NOTES:	PLATFORM: POSTS 1. 2. NOTES:	PLATFORM: POSTS 1. 2. NOTES:
THURSDAY	PLATFORM: POSTS 1. 2. NOTES:	PLATFORM: POSTS 1. 2. NOTES:	PLATFORM: POSTS 1. 2. NOTES:
FRIDAY	PLATFORM: POSTS 1. 2. NOTES:	PLATFORM: POSTS 1. 2. NOTES:	PLATFORM: POSTS 1. 2. NOTES:

	SATURDAY	SUNDAY
WEEKEND	POSTS (PLATFORM) 1. 2. NOTES:	POSTS (PLATFORM) 1. 2. NOTES:

Weekly Journal / Writing Notes

freestyle
(yourstyle)

Weekly Calendar

WEEK MONTH YEAR

Cipher: writing time | editing time | social media | administration | ______ | ______ | ______

	SUNDAY	MONDAY	TUESDAY	WEDNESDAY	THURSDAY	FRIDAY	SATURDAY
Date							
7:00 – 8:00							
8:00 – 9:00							
9:00 – 10:00							
10:00 – 11:00							
11:00 – 12:00							
12:00 – 1:00							
1:00 – 2:00							
2:00 – 3:00							
3:00 – 4:00							
4:00 – 5:00							
5:00 – 6:00							
6:00 – 7:00							
7:00 – 8:00							
8:00 – 9:00							
9:00 – 10:00							
10:00 – 11:00							

Weekly Social Media Posts

MONDAY	PLATFORM: POSTS 1. 2. NOTES:	PLATFORM: POSTS 1. 2. NOTES:	PLATFORM: POSTS 1. 2. NOTES:
TUESDAY	PLATFORM: POSTS 1. 2. NOTES:	PLATFORM: POSTS 1. 2. NOTES:	PLATFORM: POSTS 1. 2. NOTES:
WEDNESDAY	PLATFORM: POSTS 1. 2. NOTES:	PLATFORM: POSTS 1. 2. NOTES:	PLATFORM: POSTS 1. 2. NOTES:
THURSDAY	PLATFORM: POSTS 1. 2. NOTES:	PLATFORM: POSTS 1. 2. NOTES:	PLATFORM: POSTS 1. 2. NOTES:
FRIDAY	PLATFORM: POSTS 1. 2. NOTES:	PLATFORM: POSTS 1. 2. NOTES:	PLATFORM: POSTS 1. 2. NOTES:

	SATURDAY	SUNDAY
WEEKEND	POSTS (PLATFORM) 1. 2. NOTES:	POSTS (PLATFORM) 1. 2. NOTES:

Weekly Journal / Writing Notes

freestyle
(yourstyle)

Weekly Calendar

WEEK MONTH YEAR

Cipher

writing time	editing time	social media	administration			

	SUNDAY	MONDAY	TUESDAY	WEDNESDAY	THURSDAY	FRIDAY	SATURDAY
Date							
7:00 – 8:00							
8:00 – 9:00							
9:00 – 10:00							
10:00 – 11:00							
11:00 – 12:00							
12:00 – 1:00							
1:00 – 2:00							
2:00 – 3:00							
3:00 – 4:00							
4:00 – 5:00							
5:00 – 6:00							
6:00 – 7:00							
7:00 – 8:00							
8:00 – 9:00							
9:00 – 10:00							
10:00 – 11:00							

Weekly Social Media Posts

MONDAY	PLATFORM: POSTS 1. 2. NOTES:	PLATFORM: POSTS 1. 2. NOTES:	PLATFORM: POSTS 1. 2. NOTES:
TUESDAY	PLATFORM: POSTS 1. 2. NOTES:	PLATFORM: POSTS 1. 2. NOTES:	PLATFORM: POSTS 1. 2. NOTES:
WEDNESDAY	PLATFORM: POSTS 1. 2. NOTES:	PLATFORM: POSTS 1. 2. NOTES:	PLATFORM: POSTS 1. 2. NOTES:
THURSDAY	PLATFORM: POSTS 1. 2. NOTES:	PLATFORM: POSTS 1. 2. NOTES:	PLATFORM: POSTS 1. 2. NOTES:
FRIDAY	PLATFORM: POSTS 1. 2. NOTES:	PLATFORM: POSTS 1. 2. NOTES:	PLATFORM: POSTS 1. 2. NOTES:

WEEKEND

SATURDAY	SUNDAY
POSTS (PLATFORM) 1. 2. NOTES:	POSTS (PLATFORM) 1. 2. NOTES:

Weekly Journal / Writing Notes

freestyle
(yourstyle)

Weekly Calendar

WEEK MONTH YEAR

Cipher: writing time | editing time | social media | administration | | |

	SUNDAY	MONDAY	TUESDAY	WEDNESDAY	THURSDAY	FRIDAY	SATURDAY
Date							
7:00 – 8:00							
8:00 – 9:00							
9:00 – 10:00							
10:00 – 11:00							
11:00 – 12:00							
12:00 – 1:00							
1:00 – 2:00							
2:00 – 3:00							
3:00 – 4:00							
4:00 – 5:00							
5:00 – 6:00							
6:00 – 7:00							
7:00 – 8:00							
8:00 – 9:00							
9:00 – 10:00							
10:00 – 11:00							

Weekly Social Media Posts

MONDAY	PLATFORM: POSTS 1. 2. NOTES:	PLATFORM: POSTS 1. 2. NOTES:	PLATFORM: POSTS 1. 2. NOTES:
TUESDAY	PLATFORM: POSTS 1. 2. NOTES:	PLATFORM: POSTS 1. 2. NOTES:	PLATFORM: POSTS 1. 2. NOTES:
WEDNESDAY	PLATFORM: POSTS 1. 2. NOTES:	PLATFORM: POSTS 1. 2. NOTES:	PLATFORM: POSTS 1. 2. NOTES:
THURSDAY	PLATFORM: POSTS 1. 2. NOTES:	PLATFORM: POSTS 1. 2. NOTES:	PLATFORM: POSTS 1. 2. NOTES:
FRIDAY	PLATFORM: POSTS 1. 2. NOTES:	PLATFORM: POSTS 1. 2. NOTES:	PLATFORM: POSTS 1. 2. NOTES:

WEEKEND	SATURDAY	SUNDAY
	POSTS (PLATFORM) 1. 2. NOTES:	POSTS (PLATFORM) 1. 2. NOTES:

Weekly Journal / Writing Notes

freestyle
(yourstyle)

N
NW
NE
W
E
SW
SE
S
Month

Habit Tracker

	Write	Edit	Read	Post on Social Media	Scroll Through Media Feeds	Take Social Media Break	Marketing	Blog	Connected with Other Writers	Exercise	Get Outside	Self-care	Meditate							
1																				
2																				
3																				
4																				
5																				
6																				
7																				
8																				
9																				
10																				
11																				
12																				
13																				
14																				
15																				
16																				
17																				
18																				
19																				
20																				
21																				
22																				
23																				
24																				
25																				
26																				
27																				
28																				
29																				
30																				
31																				

Monthly Calendar

MONTH

YEAR

SUNDAY	MONDAY	TUESDAY	WEDNESDAY	THURSDAY	FRIDAY	SATURDAY

To-Do List

MONTH: ____________________

ITEMS CARRIED OVER FROM PREVIOUS MONTH

- [ ] ____________________ - [ ] ____________________
- [ ] ____________________ - [ ] ____________________
- [ ] ____________________ - [ ] ____________________

TOP PRIORITY

- [ ] ____________________ - [ ] ____________________
- [ ] ____________________ - [ ] ____________________
- [ ] ____________________ - [ ] ____________________
- [ ] ____________________ - [ ] ____________________

IMPORTANT

- [ ] ____________________ - [ ] ____________________
- [ ] ____________________ - [ ] ____________________
- [ ] ____________________ - [ ] ____________________
- [ ] ____________________ - [ ] ____________________

TO DO

- [ ] ____________________ - [ ] ____________________
- [ ] ____________________ - [ ] ____________________
- [ ] ____________________ - [ ] ____________________
- [ ] ____________________ - [ ] ____________________
- [ ] ____________________ - [ ] ____________________
- [ ] ____________________ - [ ] ____________________
- [ ] ____________________ - [ ] ____________________
- [ ] ____________________ - [ ] ____________________
- [ ] ____________________ - [ ] ____________________
- [ ] ____________________ - [ ] ____________________
- [ ] ____________________ - [ ] ____________________
- [ ] ____________________ - [ ] ____________________

Month's Notes

If you write one story, it may be bad; if you write a hundred, you have the odds in your favor

Month's Blog Posts

1

2

3

4

5

Weekly Calendar

WEEK MONTH YEAR

Cipher: writing time | editing time | social media | administration | ____ | ____ | ____

Date	SUNDAY	MONDAY	TUESDAY	WEDNESDAY	THURSDAY	FRIDAY	SATURDAY
7:00 – 8:00							
8:00 – 9:00							
9:00 – 10:00							
10:00 – 11:00							
11:00 – 12:00							
12:00 – 1:00							
1:00 – 2:00							
2:00 – 3:00							
3:00 – 4:00							
4:00 – 5:00							
5:00 – 6:00							
6:00 – 7:00							
7:00 – 8:00							
8:00 – 9:00							
9:00 – 10:00							
10:00 – 11:00							

Weekly Social Media Posts

Day			
MONDAY	PLATFORM: POSTS 1. 2. NOTES:	PLATFORM: POSTS 1. 2. NOTES:	PLATFORM: POSTS 1. 2. NOTES:
TUESDAY	PLATFORM: POSTS 1. 2. NOTES:	PLATFORM: POSTS 1. 2. NOTES:	PLATFORM: POSTS 1. 2. NOTES:
WEDNESDAY	PLATFORM: POSTS 1. 2. NOTES:	PLATFORM: POSTS 1. 2. NOTES:	PLATFORM: POSTS 1. 2. NOTES:
THURSDAY	PLATFORM: POSTS 1. 2. NOTES:	PLATFORM: POSTS 1. 2. NOTES:	PLATFORM: POSTS 1. 2. NOTES:
FRIDAY	PLATFORM: POSTS 1. 2. NOTES:	PLATFORM: POSTS 1. 2. NOTES:	PLATFORM: POSTS 1. 2. NOTES:

WEEKEND	SATURDAY	SUNDAY
	POSTS (PLATFORM) 1. 2. NOTES:	POSTS (PLATFORM) 1. 2. NOTES:

Weekly Journal / Writing Notes

freestyle
(yourstyle)
LOVE
BROKEN

Weekly Calendar

WEEK MONTH YEAR

Cipher: writing time | editing time | social media | administration | ___ | ___ | ___

Date	SUNDAY	MONDAY	TUESDAY	WEDNESDAY	THURSDAY	FRIDAY	SATURDAY
7:00 – 8:00							
8:00 – 9:00							
9:00 – 10:00							
10:00 – 11:00							
11:00 – 12:00							
12:00 – 1:00							
1:00 – 2:00							
2:00 – 3:00							
3:00 – 4:00							
4:00 – 5:00							
5:00 – 6:00							
6:00 – 7:00							
7:00 – 8:00							
8:00 – 9:00							
9:00 – 10:00							
10:00 – 11:00							

Weekly Social Media Posts

MONDAY	PLATFORM: POSTS 1. 2. NOTES:	PLATFORM: POSTS 1. 2. NOTES:	PLATFORM: POSTS 1. 2. NOTES:
TUESDAY	PLATFORM: POSTS 1. 2. NOTES:	PLATFORM: POSTS 1. 2. NOTES:	PLATFORM: POSTS 1. 2. NOTES:
WEDNESDAY	PLATFORM: POSTS 1. 2. NOTES:	PLATFORM: POSTS 1. 2. NOTES:	PLATFORM: POSTS 1. 2. NOTES:
THURSDAY	PLATFORM: POSTS 1. 2. NOTES:	PLATFORM: POSTS 1. 2. NOTES:	PLATFORM: POSTS 1. 2. NOTES:
FRIDAY	PLATFORM: POSTS 1. 2. NOTES:	PLATFORM: POSTS 1. 2. NOTES:	PLATFORM: POSTS 1. 2. NOTES:

WEEKEND	SATURDAY	SUNDAY
	POSTS (PLATFORM) 1. 2. NOTES:	POSTS (PLATFORM) 1. 2. NOTES:

Weekly Journal / Writing Notes

freestyle
(yourstyle)

Weekly Calendar

WEEK MONTH YEAR

Cipher: writing time | editing time | social media | administration | ____ | ____ | ____

Date	SUNDAY	MONDAY	TUESDAY	WEDNESDAY	THURSDAY	FRIDAY	SATURDAY
7:00 – 8:00							
8:00 – 9:00							
9:00 – 10:00							
10:00 – 11:00							
11:00 – 12:00							
12:00 – 1:00							
1:00 – 2:00							
2:00 – 3:00							
3:00 – 4:00							
4:00 – 5:00							
5:00 – 6:00							
6:00 – 7:00							
7:00 – 8:00							
8:00 – 9:00							
9:00 – 10:00							
10:00 – 11:00							

Weekly Social Media Posts

MONDAY	PLATFORM: POSTS 1. 2. NOTES:	PLATFORM: POSTS 1. 2. NOTES:	PLATFORM: POSTS 1. 2. NOTES:
TUESDAY	PLATFORM: POSTS 1. 2. NOTES:	PLATFORM: POSTS 1. 2. NOTES:	PLATFORM: POSTS 1. 2. NOTES:
WEDNESDAY	PLATFORM: POSTS 1. 2. NOTES:	PLATFORM: POSTS 1. 2. NOTES:	PLATFORM: POSTS 1. 2. NOTES:
THURSDAY	PLATFORM: POSTS 1. 2. NOTES:	PLATFORM: POSTS 1. 2. NOTES:	PLATFORM: POSTS 1. 2. NOTES:
FRIDAY	PLATFORM: POSTS 1. 2. NOTES:	PLATFORM: POSTS 1. 2. NOTES:	PLATFORM: POSTS 1. 2. NOTES:

WEEKEND	SATURDAY	SUNDAY
	POSTS (PLATFORM) 1. 2. NOTES:	POSTS (PLATFORM) 1. 2. NOTES:

Weekly Journal / Writing Notes

freestyle
(yourstyle)

Weekly Calendar

WEEK MONTH YEAR

Cipher

writing time | editing time | social media | administration

	SUNDAY	MONDAY	TUESDAY	WEDNESDAY	THURSDAY	FRIDAY	SATURDAY
Date							
7:00 – 8:00							
8:00 – 9:00							
9:00 – 10:00							
10:00 – 11:00							
11:00 – 12:00							
12:00 – 1:00							
1:00 – 2:00							
2:00 – 3:00							
3:00 – 4:00							
4:00 – 5:00							
5:00 – 6:00							
6:00 – 7:00							
7:00 – 8:00							
8:00 – 9:00							
9:00 – 10:00							
10:00 – 11:00							

Weekly Social Media Posts

MONDAY	PLATFORM: POSTS 1. 2. NOTES:	PLATFORM: POSTS 1. 2. NOTES:	PLATFORM: POSTS 1. 2. NOTES:
TUESDAY	PLATFORM: POSTS 1. 2. NOTES:	PLATFORM: POSTS 1. 2. NOTES:	PLATFORM: POSTS 1. 2. NOTES:
WEDNESDAY	PLATFORM: POSTS 1. 2. NOTES:	PLATFORM: POSTS 1. 2. NOTES:	PLATFORM: POSTS 1. 2. NOTES:
THURSDAY	PLATFORM: POSTS 1. 2. NOTES:	PLATFORM: POSTS 1. 2. NOTES:	PLATFORM: POSTS 1. 2. NOTES:
FRIDAY	PLATFORM: POSTS 1. 2. NOTES:	PLATFORM: POSTS 1. 2. NOTES:	PLATFORM: POSTS 1. 2. NOTES:

WEEKEND	SATURDAY	SUNDAY
	POSTS (PLATFORM) 1. 2. NOTES:	POSTS (PLATFORM) 1. 2. NOTES:

Weekly Journal / Writing Notes

freestyle
(yourstyle)

Weekly Calendar

WEEK MONTH YEAR

Cipher

writing time | editing time | social media | administration

Date	SUNDAY	MONDAY	TUESDAY	WEDNESDAY	THURSDAY	FRIDAY	SATURDAY
7:00 – 8:00							
8:00 – 9:00							
9:00 – 10:00							
10:00 – 11:00							
11:00 – 12:00							
12:00 – 1:00							
1:00 – 2:00							
2:00 – 3:00							
3:00 – 4:00							
4:00 – 5:00							
5:00 – 6:00							
6:00 – 7:00							
7:00 – 8:00							
8:00 – 9:00							
9:00 – 10:00							
10:00 – 11:00							

Weekly Social Media Posts

MONDAY	PLATFORM: POSTS 1. 2. NOTES:	PLATFORM: POSTS 1. 2. NOTES:	PLATFORM: POSTS 1. 2. NOTES:
TUESDAY	PLATFORM: POSTS 1. 2. NOTES:	PLATFORM: POSTS 1. 2. NOTES:	PLATFORM: POSTS 1. 2. NOTES:
WEDNESDAY	PLATFORM: POSTS 1. 2. NOTES:	PLATFORM: POSTS 1. 2. NOTES:	PLATFORM: POSTS 1. 2. NOTES:
THURSDAY	PLATFORM: POSTS 1. 2. NOTES:	PLATFORM: POSTS 1. 2. NOTES:	PLATFORM: POSTS 1. 2. NOTES:
FRIDAY	PLATFORM: POSTS 1. 2. NOTES:	PLATFORM: POSTS 1. 2. NOTES:	PLATFORM: POSTS 1. 2. NOTES:

WEEKEND	SATURDAY	SUNDAY
	POSTS (PLATFORM) 1. 2. NOTES:	POSTS (PLATFORM) 1. 2. NOTES:

Weekly Journal / Writing Notes

freestyle
(yourstyle)

Month

____

Habit Tracker

	Write	Edit	Read	Post on Social Media	Scroll Through Media Feeds	Take Social Media Break	Marketing	Blog	Connected with Other Writers	Exercise	Get Outside	Self-care	Meditate							
1																				
2																				
3																				
4																				
5																				
6																				
7																				
8																				
9																				
10																				
11																				
12																				
13																				
14																				
15																				
16																				
17																				
18																				
19																				
20																				
21																				
22																				
23																				
24																				
25																				
26																				
27																				
28																				
29																				
30																				
31																				

Monthly Calendar

MONTH YEAR

SUNDAY	MONDAY	TUESDAY	WEDNESDAY	THURSDAY	FRIDAY	SATURDAY

To-Do List

MONTH: ______________________

ITEMS CARRIED OVER FROM PREVIOUS MONTH

- [ ] ______________________ - [ ] ______________________
- [ ] ______________________ - [ ] ______________________
- [ ] ______________________ - [ ] ______________________

TOP PRIORITY

- [ ] ______________________ - [ ] ______________________
- [ ] ______________________ - [ ] ______________________
- [ ] ______________________ - [ ] ______________________
- [ ] ______________________ - [ ] ______________________

IMPORTANT

- [ ] ______________________ - [ ] ______________________
- [ ] ______________________ - [ ] ______________________
- [ ] ______________________ - [ ] ______________________
- [ ] ______________________ - [ ] ______________________

TO DO

- [ ] ______________________ - [ ] ______________________
- [ ] ______________________ - [ ] ______________________
- [ ] ______________________ - [ ] ______________________
- [ ] ______________________ - [ ] ______________________
- [ ] ______________________ - [ ] ______________________
- [ ] ______________________ - [ ] ______________________
- [ ] ______________________ - [ ] ______________________
- [ ] ______________________ - [ ] ______________________
- [ ] ______________________ - [ ] ______________________
- [ ] ______________________ - [ ] ______________________
- [ ] ______________________ - [ ] ______________________
- [ ] ______________________ - [ ] ______________________

Month's Notes

Month's Blog Posts

1

2

3

4

5

Weekly Calendar

WEEK MONTH YEAR

Cipher

writing time	editing time	social media	administration			

	SUNDAY	MONDAY	TUESDAY	WEDNESDAY	THURSDAY	FRIDAY	SATURDAY
Date							
7:00 – 8:00							
8:00 – 9:00							
9:00 – 10:00							
10:00 – 11:00							
11:00 – 12:00							
12:00 – 1:00							
1:00 – 2:00							
2:00 – 3:00							
3:00 – 4:00							
4:00 – 5:00							
5:00 – 6:00							
6:00 – 7:00							
7:00 – 8:00							
8:00 – 9:00							
9:00 – 10:00							
10:00 – 11:00							

Weekly Social Media Posts

MONDAY	PLATFORM: POSTS 1. 2. NOTES:	PLATFORM: POSTS 1. 2. NOTES:	PLATFORM: POSTS 1. 2. NOTES:
TUESDAY	PLATFORM: POSTS 1. 2. NOTES:	PLATFORM: POSTS 1. 2. NOTES:	PLATFORM: POSTS 1. 2. NOTES:
WEDNESDAY	PLATFORM: POSTS 1. 2. NOTES:	PLATFORM: POSTS 1. 2. NOTES:	PLATFORM: POSTS 1. 2. NOTES:
THURSDAY	PLATFORM: POSTS 1. 2. NOTES:	PLATFORM: POSTS 1. 2. NOTES:	PLATFORM: POSTS 1. 2. NOTES:
FRIDAY	PLATFORM: POSTS 1. 2. NOTES:	PLATFORM: POSTS 1. 2. NOTES:	PLATFORM: POSTS 1. 2. NOTES:

WEEKEND	SATURDAY	SUNDAY
	POSTS (PLATFORM) 1. 2. NOTES:	POSTS (PLATFORM) 1. 2. NOTES:

Weekly Journal / Writing Notes

freestyle
(yourstyle)
LOVE
BROKEN

Weekly Calendar

WEEK MONTH YEAR

Cipher: writing time | editing time | social media | administration | ___ | ___ | ___

Date	SUNDAY	MONDAY	TUESDAY	WEDNESDAY	THURSDAY	FRIDAY	SATURDAY
7:00 – 8:00							
8:00 – 9:00							
9:00 – 10:00							
10:00 – 11:00							
11:00 – 12:00							
12:00 – 1:00							
1:00 – 2:00							
2:00 – 3:00							
3:00 – 4:00							
4:00 – 5:00							
5:00 – 6:00							
6:00 – 7:00							
7:00 – 8:00							
8:00 – 9:00							
9:00 – 10:00							
10:00 – 11:00							

Weekly Social Media Posts

MONDAY	PLATFORM: POSTS 1. 2. NOTES:	PLATFORM: POSTS 1. 2. NOTES:	PLATFORM: POSTS 1. 2. NOTES:
TUESDAY	PLATFORM: POSTS 1. 2. NOTES:	PLATFORM: POSTS 1. 2. NOTES:	PLATFORM: POSTS 1. 2. NOTES:
WEDNESDAY	PLATFORM: POSTS 1. 2. NOTES:	PLATFORM: POSTS 1. 2. NOTES:	PLATFORM: POSTS 1. 2. NOTES:
THURSDAY	PLATFORM: POSTS 1. 2. NOTES:	PLATFORM: POSTS 1. 2. NOTES:	PLATFORM: POSTS 1. 2. NOTES:
FRIDAY	PLATFORM: POSTS 1. 2. NOTES:	PLATFORM: POSTS 1. 2. NOTES:	PLATFORM: POSTS 1. 2. NOTES:

WEEKEND	SATURDAY POSTS (PLATFORM) 1. 2. NOTES:	SUNDAY POSTS (PLATFORM) 1. 2. NOTES:

Weekly Journal / Writing Notes

freestyle
(yourstyle)

Weekly Calendar

WEEK MONTH YEAR

Cipher: writing time, editing time, social media, administration

	SUNDAY	MONDAY	TUESDAY	WEDNESDAY	THURSDAY	FRIDAY	SATURDAY
Date							
7:00 – 8:00							
8:00 – 9:00							
9:00 – 10:00							
10:00 – 11:00							
11:00 – 12:00							
12:00 – 1:00							
1:00 – 2:00							
2:00 – 3:00							
3:00 – 4:00							
4:00 – 5:00							
5:00 – 6:00							
6:00 – 7:00							
7:00 – 8:00							
8:00 – 9:00							
9:00 – 10:00							
10:00 – 11:00							

Weekly Social Media Posts

MONDAY	PLATFORM: POSTS 1. 2. NOTES:	PLATFORM: POSTS 1. 2. NOTES:	PLATFORM: POSTS 1. 2. NOTES:
TUESDAY	PLATFORM: POSTS 1. 2. NOTES:	PLATFORM: POSTS 1. 2. NOTES:	PLATFORM: POSTS 1. 2. NOTES:
WEDNESDAY	PLATFORM: POSTS 1. 2. NOTES:	PLATFORM: POSTS 1. 2. NOTES:	PLATFORM: POSTS 1. 2. NOTES:
THURSDAY	PLATFORM: POSTS 1. 2. NOTES:	PLATFORM: POSTS 1. 2. NOTES:	PLATFORM: POSTS 1. 2. NOTES:
FRIDAY	PLATFORM: POSTS 1. 2. NOTES:	PLATFORM: POSTS 1. 2. NOTES:	PLATFORM: POSTS 1. 2. NOTES:

WEEKEND	SATURDAY	SUNDAY
	POSTS (PLATFORM) 1. 2. NOTES:	POSTS (PLATFORM) 1. 2. NOTES:

Weekly Journal / Writing Notes

freestyle
(yourstyle)

Weekly Calendar

WEEK MONTH YEAR

Cipher: writing time | editing time | social media | administration

	SUNDAY	MONDAY	TUESDAY	WEDNESDAY	THURSDAY	FRIDAY	SATURDAY
Date							
7:00 – 8:00							
8:00 – 9:00							
9:00 – 10:00							
10:00 – 11:00							
11:00 – 12:00							
12:00 – 1:00							
1:00 – 2:00							
2:00 – 3:00							
3:00 – 4:00							
4:00 – 5:00							
5:00 – 6:00							
6:00 – 7:00							
7:00 – 8:00							
8:00 – 9:00							
9:00 – 10:00							
10:00 – 11:00							

Weekly Social Media Posts

MONDAY	PLATFORM: POSTS 1. 2. NOTES:	PLATFORM: POSTS 1. 2. NOTES:	PLATFORM: POSTS 1. 2. NOTES:
TUESDAY	PLATFORM: POSTS 1. 2. NOTES:	PLATFORM: POSTS 1. 2. NOTES:	PLATFORM: POSTS 1. 2. NOTES:
WEDNESDAY	PLATFORM: POSTS 1. 2. NOTES:	PLATFORM: POSTS 1. 2. NOTES:	PLATFORM: POSTS 1. 2. NOTES:
THURSDAY	PLATFORM: POSTS 1. 2. NOTES:	PLATFORM: POSTS 1. 2. NOTES:	PLATFORM: POSTS 1. 2. NOTES:
FRIDAY	PLATFORM: POSTS 1. 2. NOTES:	PLATFORM: POSTS 1. 2. NOTES:	PLATFORM: POSTS 1. 2. NOTES:

	SATURDAY	SUNDAY
WEEKEND	POSTS (PLATFORM) 1. 2. NOTES:	POSTS (PLATFORM) 1. 2. NOTES:

Weekly Journal / Writing Notes

freestyle
(yourstyle)

Weekly Calendar

WEEK MONTH YEAR

Cipher: writing time | editing time | social media | administration | ____ | ____ | ____

	SUNDAY	MONDAY	TUESDAY	WEDNESDAY	THURSDAY	FRIDAY	SATURDAY
Date							
7:00 – 8:00							
8:00 – 9:00							
9:00 – 10:00							
10:00 – 11:00							
11:00 – 12:00							
12:00 – 1:00							
1:00 – 2:00							
2:00 – 3:00							
3:00 – 4:00							
4:00 – 5:00							
5:00 – 6:00							
6:00 – 7:00							
7:00 – 8:00							
8:00 – 9:00							
9:00 – 10:00							
10:00 – 11:00							

Weekly Social Media Posts

MONDAY	PLATFORM: POSTS 1. 2. NOTES:	PLATFORM: POSTS 1. 2. NOTES:	PLATFORM: POSTS 1. 2. NOTES:
TUESDAY	PLATFORM: POSTS 1. 2. NOTES:	PLATFORM: POSTS 1. 2. NOTES:	PLATFORM: POSTS 1. 2. NOTES:
WEDNESDAY	PLATFORM: POSTS 1. 2. NOTES:	PLATFORM: POSTS 1. 2. NOTES:	PLATFORM: POSTS 1. 2. NOTES:
THURSDAY	PLATFORM: POSTS 1. 2. NOTES:	PLATFORM: POSTS 1. 2. NOTES:	PLATFORM: POSTS 1. 2. NOTES:
FRIDAY	PLATFORM: POSTS 1. 2. NOTES:	PLATFORM: POSTS 1. 2. NOTES:	PLATFORM: POSTS 1. 2. NOTES:
WEEKEND	SATURDAY POSTS (PLATFORM) 1. 2. NOTES:	SUNDAY POSTS (PLATFORM) 1. 2. NOTES:	

Weekly Journal / Writing Notes

freestyle
(yourstyle)

Month

Habit Tracker

	Write	Edit	Read	Post on Social Media	Scroll Through Media Feeds	Take Social Media Break	Marketing	Blog	Connected with Other Writers	Exercise	Get Outside	Self-care	Meditate							
1																				
2																				
3																				
4																				
5																				
6																				
7																				
8																				
9																				
10																				
11																				
12																				
13																				
14																				
15																				
16																				
17																				
18																				
19																				
20																				
21																				
22																				
23																				
24																				
25																				
26																				
27																				
28																				
29																				
30																				
31																				

Monthly Calendar

MONTH YEAR

SUNDAY	MONDAY	TUESDAY	WEDNESDAY	THURSDAY	FRIDAY	SATURDAY

To-Do List

MONTH: ____________________

ITEMS CARRIED OVER FROM PREVIOUS MONTH

- [ ] ____________________
- [ ] ____________________
- [ ] ____________________
- [ ] ____________________
- [ ] ____________________
- [ ] ____________________

TOP PRIORITY

- [ ] ____________________
- [ ] ____________________
- [ ] ____________________
- [ ] ____________________
- [ ] ____________________
- [ ] ____________________
- [ ] ____________________
- [ ] ____________________

IMPORTANT

- [ ] ____________________
- [ ] ____________________
- [ ] ____________________
- [ ] ____________________
- [ ] ____________________
- [ ] ____________________
- [ ] ____________________
- [ ] ____________________

TO DO

- [ ] ____________________
- [ ] ____________________
- [ ] ____________________
- [ ] ____________________
- [ ] ____________________
- [ ] ____________________
- [ ] ____________________
- [ ] ____________________
- [ ] ____________________
- [ ] ____________________
- [ ] ____________________
- [ ] ____________________
- [ ] ____________________
- [ ] ____________________
- [ ] ____________________
- [ ] ____________________
- [ ] ____________________
- [ ] ____________________
- [ ] ____________________
- [ ] ____________________
- [ ] ____________________
- [ ] ____________________
- [ ] ____________________
- [ ] ____________________

Start writing
no matter what
The water doesn't flow
until the
faucet is Turned ON

Month's Notes

Month's Blog Posts

1

2

3

4

5

Weekly Calendar

WEEK MONTH YEAR

Cipher: writing time | editing time | social media | administration | ____ | ____ | ____

	SUNDAY	MONDAY	TUESDAY	WEDNESDAY	THURSDAY	FRIDAY	SATURDAY
Date							
7:00 – 8:00							
8:00 – 9:00							
9:00 – 10:00							
10:00 – 11:00							
11:00 – 12:00							
12:00 – 1:00							
1:00 – 2:00							
2:00 – 3:00							
3:00 – 4:00							
4:00 – 5:00							
5:00 – 6:00							
6:00 – 7:00							
7:00 – 8:00							
8:00 – 9:00							
9:00 – 10:00							
10:00 – 11:00							

Weekly Social Media Posts

MONDAY	PLATFORM: POSTS 1. 2. NOTES:	PLATFORM: POSTS 1. 2. NOTES:	PLATFORM: POSTS 1. 2. NOTES:
TUESDAY	PLATFORM: POSTS 1. 2. NOTES:	PLATFORM: POSTS 1. 2. NOTES:	PLATFORM: POSTS 1. 2. NOTES:
WEDNESDAY	PLATFORM: POSTS 1. 2. NOTES:	PLATFORM: POSTS 1. 2. NOTES:	PLATFORM: POSTS 1. 2. NOTES:
THURSDAY	PLATFORM: POSTS 1. 2. NOTES:	PLATFORM: POSTS 1. 2. NOTES:	PLATFORM: POSTS 1. 2. NOTES:
FRIDAY	PLATFORM: POSTS 1. 2. NOTES:	PLATFORM: POSTS 1. 2. NOTES:	PLATFORM: POSTS 1. 2. NOTES:

	SATURDAY	SUNDAY
WEEKEND	POSTS (PLATFORM) 1. 2. NOTES:	POSTS (PLATFORM) 1. 2. NOTES:

Weekly Journal / Writing Notes

freestyle
(yourstyle)
LOVE
BROKEN

Weekly Calendar

WEEK MONTH YEAR

Cipher: writing time, editing time, social media, administration, ____, ____, ____

	SUNDAY	MONDAY	TUESDAY	WEDNESDAY	THURSDAY	FRIDAY	SATURDAY
Date							
7:00 – 8:00							
8:00 – 9:00							
9:00 – 10:00							
10:00 – 11:00							
11:00 – 12:00							
12:00 – 1:00							
1:00 – 2:00							
2:00 – 3:00							
3:00 – 4:00							
4:00 – 5:00							
5:00 – 6:00							
6:00 – 7:00							
7:00 – 8:00							
8:00 – 9:00							
9:00 – 10:00							
10:00 – 11:00							

Weekly Social Media Posts

MONDAY	PLATFORM: POSTS 1. 2. NOTES:	PLATFORM: POSTS 1. 2. NOTES:	PLATFORM: POSTS 1. 2. NOTES:
TUESDAY	PLATFORM: POSTS 1. 2. NOTES:	PLATFORM: POSTS 1. 2. NOTES:	PLATFORM: POSTS 1. 2. NOTES:
WEDNESDAY	PLATFORM: POSTS 1. 2. NOTES:	PLATFORM: POSTS 1. 2. NOTES:	PLATFORM: POSTS 1. 2. NOTES:
THURSDAY	PLATFORM: POSTS 1. 2. NOTES:	PLATFORM: POSTS 1. 2. NOTES:	PLATFORM: POSTS 1. 2. NOTES:
FRIDAY	PLATFORM: POSTS 1. 2. NOTES:	PLATFORM: POSTS 1. 2. NOTES:	PLATFORM: POSTS 1. 2. NOTES:

WEEKEND	SATURDAY	SUNDAY
	POSTS (PLATFORM) 1. 2. NOTES:	POSTS (PLATFORM) 1. 2. NOTES:

Weekly Journal / Writing Notes

freestyle
(yourstyle)

Weekly Calendar

WEEK MONTH YEAR

Cipher

writing time	editing time	social media	administration			

	SUNDAY	MONDAY	TUESDAY	WEDNESDAY	THURSDAY	FRIDAY	SATURDAY
Date							
7:00 – 8:00							
8:00 – 9:00							
9:00 – 10:00							
10:00 – 11:00							
11:00 – 12:00							
12:00 – 1:00							
1:00 – 2:00							
2:00 – 3:00							
3:00 – 4:00							
4:00 – 5:00							
5:00 – 6:00							
6:00 – 7:00							
7:00 – 8:00							
8:00 – 9:00							
9:00 – 10:00							
10:00 – 11:00							

Weekly Social Media Posts

MONDAY	PLATFORM: POSTS 1. 2. NOTES:	PLATFORM: POSTS 1. 2. NOTES:	PLATFORM: POSTS 1. 2. NOTES:
TUESDAY	PLATFORM: POSTS 1. 2. NOTES:	PLATFORM: POSTS 1. 2. NOTES:	PLATFORM: POSTS 1. 2. NOTES:
WEDNESDAY	PLATFORM: POSTS 1. 2. NOTES:	PLATFORM: POSTS 1. 2. NOTES:	PLATFORM: POSTS 1. 2. NOTES:
THURSDAY	PLATFORM: POSTS 1. 2. NOTES:	PLATFORM: POSTS 1. 2. NOTES:	PLATFORM: POSTS 1. 2. NOTES:
FRIDAY	PLATFORM: POSTS 1. 2. NOTES:	PLATFORM: POSTS 1. 2. NOTES:	PLATFORM: POSTS 1. 2. NOTES:

WEEKEND	SATURDAY POSTS (PLATFORM) 1. 2. NOTES:	SUNDAY POSTS (PLATFORM) 1. 2. NOTES:

Weekly Journal / Writing Notes

freestyle
(yourstyle)

Weekly Calendar

WEEK MONTH YEAR

Cipher: writing time | editing time | social media | administration | ____ | ____ | ____

	SUNDAY	MONDAY	TUESDAY	WEDNESDAY	THURSDAY	FRIDAY	SATURDAY
Date							
7:00 – 8:00							
8:00 – 9:00							
9:00 – 10:00							
10:00 – 11:00							
11:00 – 12:00							
12:00 – 1:00							
1:00 – 2:00							
2:00 – 3:00							
3:00 – 4:00							
4:00 – 5:00							
5:00 – 6:00							
6:00 – 7:00							
7:00 – 8:00							
8:00 – 9:00							
9:00 – 10:00							
10:00 – 11:00							

Weekly Social Media Posts

MONDAY	PLATFORM: POSTS 1. 2. NOTES:	PLATFORM: POSTS 1. 2. NOTES:	PLATFORM: POSTS 1. 2. NOTES:
TUESDAY	PLATFORM: POSTS 1. 2. NOTES:	PLATFORM: POSTS 1. 2. NOTES:	PLATFORM: POSTS 1. 2. NOTES:
WEDNESDAY	PLATFORM: POSTS 1. 2. NOTES:	PLATFORM: POSTS 1. 2. NOTES:	PLATFORM: POSTS 1. 2. NOTES:
THURSDAY	PLATFORM: POSTS 1. 2. NOTES:	PLATFORM: POSTS 1. 2. NOTES:	PLATFORM: POSTS 1. 2. NOTES:
FRIDAY	PLATFORM: POSTS 1. 2. NOTES:	PLATFORM: POSTS 1. 2. NOTES:	PLATFORM: POSTS 1. 2. NOTES:

	SATURDAY	SUNDAY
WEEKEND	POSTS (PLATFORM) 1. 2. NOTES:	POSTS (PLATFORM) 1. 2. NOTES:

Weekly Journal / Writing Notes

freestyle
(yourstyle)

Weekly Calendar

WEEK MONTH YEAR

Cipher: writing time | editing time | social media | administration | ____ | ____ | ____

Date	SUNDAY	MONDAY	TUESDAY	WEDNESDAY	THURSDAY	FRIDAY	SATURDAY
7:00 – 8:00							
8:00 – 9:00							
9:00 – 10:00							
10:00 – 11:00							
11:00 – 12:00							
12:00 – 1:00							
1:00 – 2:00							
2:00 – 3:00							
3:00 – 4:00							
4:00 – 5:00							
5:00 – 6:00							
6:00 – 7:00							
7:00 – 8:00							
8:00 – 9:00							
9:00 – 10:00							
10:00 – 11:00							

Weekly Social Media Posts

MONDAY	PLATFORM: POSTS 1. 2. NOTES:	PLATFORM: POSTS 1. 2. NOTES:	PLATFORM: POSTS 1. 2. NOTES:
TUESDAY	PLATFORM: POSTS 1. 2. NOTES:	PLATFORM: POSTS 1. 2. NOTES:	PLATFORM: POSTS 1. 2. NOTES:
WEDNESDAY	PLATFORM: POSTS 1. 2. NOTES:	PLATFORM: POSTS 1. 2. NOTES:	PLATFORM: POSTS 1. 2. NOTES:
THURSDAY	PLATFORM: POSTS 1. 2. NOTES:	PLATFORM: POSTS 1. 2. NOTES:	PLATFORM: POSTS 1. 2. NOTES:
FRIDAY	PLATFORM: POSTS 1. 2. NOTES:	PLATFORM: POSTS 1. 2. NOTES:	PLATFORM: POSTS 1. 2. NOTES:
WEEKEND	SATURDAY POSTS (PLATFORM) 1. 2. NOTES:	SUNDAY POSTS (PLATFORM) 1. 2. NOTES:	

Weekly Journal / Writing Notes

freestyle
(yourstyle)

Month

____

Habit Tracker

	Write	Edit	Read	Post on Social Media	Scroll Through Media Feeds	Take Social Media Break	Marketing	Blog	Connected with Other Writers	Exercise	Get Outside	Self-care	Meditate							
1																				
2																				
3																				
4																				
5																				
6																				
7																				
8																				
9																				
10																				
11																				
12																				
13																				
14																				
15																				
16																				
17																				
18																				
19																				
20																				
21																				
22																				
23																				
24																				
25																				
26																				
27																				
28																				
29																				
30																				
31																				

Monthly Calendar

MONTH YEAR

SUNDAY	MONDAY	TUESDAY	WEDNESDAY	THURSDAY	FRIDAY	SATURDAY

To-Do List

MONTH: ______________________________

ITEMS CARRIED OVER FROM PREVIEOUS MONTH

- [ ] ______________________ - [ ] ______________________
- [ ] ______________________ - [ ] ______________________
- [ ] ______________________ - [ ] ______________________

TOP PRIORITY

- [ ] ______________________ - [ ] ______________________
- [ ] ______________________ - [ ] ______________________
- [ ] ______________________ - [ ] ______________________
- [ ] ______________________ - [ ] ______________________

IMPORTANT

- [ ] ______________________ - [ ] ______________________
- [ ] ______________________ - [ ] ______________________
- [ ] ______________________ - [ ] ______________________
- [ ] ______________________ - [ ] ______________________

TO DO

- [ ] ______________________ - [ ] ______________________
- [ ] ______________________ - [ ] ______________________
- [ ] ______________________ - [ ] ______________________
- [ ] ______________________ - [ ] ______________________
- [ ] ______________________ - [ ] ______________________
- [ ] ______________________ - [ ] ______________________
- [ ] ______________________ - [ ] ______________________
- [ ] ______________________ - [ ] ______________________
- [ ] ______________________ - [ ] ______________________
- [ ] ______________________ - [ ] ______________________
- [ ] ______________________ - [ ] ______________________
- [ ] ______________________ - [ ] ______________________

Month's Notes

Month's Blog Posts

1

2

3

4

5

Weekly Calendar

WEEK MONTH YEAR

Cipher

writing time	editing time	social media	administration			

	SUNDAY	MONDAY	TUESDAY	WEDNESDAY	THURSDAY	FRIDAY	SATURDAY
Date							
7:00 – 8:00							
8:00 – 9:00							
9:00 – 10:00							
10:00 – 11:00							
11:00 – 12:00							
12:00 – 1:00							
1:00 – 2:00							
2:00 – 3:00							
3:00 – 4:00							
4:00 – 5:00							
5:00 – 6:00							
6:00 – 7:00							
7:00 – 8:00							
8:00 – 9:00							
9:00 – 10:00							
10:00 – 11:00							

Weekly Social Media Posts

MONDAY	PLATFORM: POSTS 1. 2. NOTES:	PLATFORM: POSTS 1. 2. NOTES:	PLATFORM: POSTS 1. 2. NOTES:
TUESDAY	PLATFORM: POSTS 1. 2. NOTES:	PLATFORM: POSTS 1. 2. NOTES:	PLATFORM: POSTS 1. 2. NOTES:
WEDNESDAY	PLATFORM: POSTS 1. 2. NOTES:	PLATFORM: POSTS 1. 2. NOTES:	PLATFORM: POSTS 1. 2. NOTES:
THURSDAY	PLATFORM: POSTS 1. 2. NOTES:	PLATFORM: POSTS 1. 2. NOTES:	PLATFORM: POSTS 1. 2. NOTES:
FRIDAY	PLATFORM: POSTS 1. 2. NOTES:	PLATFORM: POSTS 1. 2. NOTES:	PLATFORM: POSTS 1. 2. NOTES:

WEEKEND	SATURDAY	SUNDAY
	POSTS (PLATFORM) 1. 2. NOTES:	POSTS (PLATFORM) 1. 2. NOTES:

Weekly Journal / Writing Notes

freestyle
(yourstyle)
LOVE
BROKEN

Weekly Calendar

WEEK MONTH YEAR

Cipher

writing time | editing time | social media | administration

	SUNDAY	MONDAY	TUESDAY	WEDNESDAY	THURSDAY	FRIDAY	SATURDAY
Date							
7:00 – 8:00							
8:00 – 9:00							
9:00 – 10:00							
10:00 – 11:00							
11:00 – 12:00							
12:00 – 1:00							
1:00 – 2:00							
2:00 – 3:00							
3:00 – 4:00							
4:00 – 5:00							
5:00 – 6:00							
6:00 – 7:00							
7:00 – 8:00							
8:00 – 9:00							
9:00 – 10:00							
10:00 – 11:00							

Weekly Social Media Posts

MONDAY	PLATFORM: POSTS 1. 2. NOTES:	PLATFORM: POSTS 1. 2. NOTES:	PLATFORM: POSTS 1. 2. NOTES:
TUESDAY	PLATFORM: POSTS 1. 2. NOTES:	PLATFORM: POSTS 1. 2. NOTES:	PLATFORM: POSTS 1. 2. NOTES:
WEDNESDAY	PLATFORM: POSTS 1. 2. NOTES:	PLATFORM: POSTS 1. 2. NOTES:	PLATFORM: POSTS 1. 2. NOTES:
THURSDAY	PLATFORM: POSTS 1. 2. NOTES:	PLATFORM: POSTS 1. 2. NOTES:	PLATFORM: POSTS 1. 2. NOTES:
FRIDAY	PLATFORM: POSTS 1. 2. NOTES:	PLATFORM: POSTS 1. 2. NOTES:	PLATFORM: POSTS 1. 2. NOTES:

WEEKEND	SATURDAY	SUNDAY
	POSTS (PLATFORM) 1. 2. NOTES:	POSTS (PLATFORM) 1. 2. NOTES:

Weekly Journal / Writing Notes

freestyle
(yourstyle)

Weekly Calendar

WEEK MONTH YEAR

Cipher

writing time	editing time	social media	administration			

	SUNDAY	MONDAY	TUESDAY	WEDNESDAY	THURSDAY	FRIDAY	SATURDAY
Date							
7:00 – 8:00							
8:00 – 9:00							
9:00 – 10:00							
10:00 – 11:00							
11:00 – 12:00							
12:00 – 1:00							
1:00 – 2:00							
2:00 – 3:00							
3:00 – 4:00							
4:00 – 5:00							
5:00 – 6:00							
6:00 – 7:00							
7:00 – 8:00							
8:00 – 9:00							
9:00 – 10:00							
10:00 – 11:00							

Weekly Social Media Posts

Day			
MONDAY	PLATFORM: POSTS 1. 2. NOTES:	PLATFORM: POSTS 1. 2. NOTES:	PLATFORM: POSTS 1. 2. NOTES:
TUESDAY	PLATFORM: POSTS 1. 2. NOTES:	PLATFORM: POSTS 1. 2. NOTES:	PLATFORM: POSTS 1. 2. NOTES:
WEDNESDAY	PLATFORM: POSTS 1. 2. NOTES:	PLATFORM: POSTS 1. 2. NOTES:	PLATFORM: POSTS 1. 2. NOTES:
THURSDAY	PLATFORM: POSTS 1. 2. NOTES:	PLATFORM: POSTS 1. 2. NOTES:	PLATFORM: POSTS 1. 2. NOTES:
FRIDAY	PLATFORM: POSTS 1. 2. NOTES:	PLATFORM: POSTS 1. 2. NOTES:	PLATFORM: POSTS 1. 2. NOTES:

WEEKEND	SATURDAY	SUNDAY
	POSTS (PLATFORM) 1. 2. NOTES:	POSTS (PLATFORM) 1. 2. NOTES:

Weekly Journal / Writing Notes

freestyle
(yourstyle)

Weekly Calendar

WEEK MONTH YEAR

Cipher: writing time, editing time, social media, administration

	SUNDAY	MONDAY	TUESDAY	WEDNESDAY	THURSDAY	FRIDAY	SATURDAY
Date							
7:00 – 8:00							
8:00 – 9:00							
9:00 – 10:00							
10:00 – 11:00							
11:00 – 12:00							
12:00 – 1:00							
1:00 – 2:00							
2:00 – 3:00							
3:00 – 4:00							
4:00 – 5:00							
5:00 – 6:00							
6:00 – 7:00							
7:00 – 8:00							
8:00 – 9:00							
9:00 – 10:00							
10:00 – 11:00							

Weekly Social Media Posts

MONDAY	PLATFORM: POSTS 1. 2. NOTES:	PLATFORM: POSTS 1. 2. NOTES:	PLATFORM: POSTS 1. 2. NOTES:
TUESDAY	PLATFORM: POSTS 1. 2. NOTES:	PLATFORM: POSTS 1. 2. NOTES:	PLATFORM: POSTS 1. 2. NOTES:
WEDNESDAY	PLATFORM: POSTS 1. 2. NOTES:	PLATFORM: POSTS 1. 2. NOTES:	PLATFORM: POSTS 1. 2. NOTES:
THURSDAY	PLATFORM: POSTS 1. 2. NOTES:	PLATFORM: POSTS 1. 2. NOTES:	PLATFORM: POSTS 1. 2. NOTES:
FRIDAY	PLATFORM: POSTS 1. 2. NOTES:	PLATFORM: POSTS 1. 2. NOTES:	PLATFORM: POSTS 1. 2. NOTES:

WEEKEND	SATURDAY	SUNDAY
	POSTS (PLATFORM) 1. 2. NOTES:	POSTS (PLATFORM) 1. 2. NOTES:

Weekly Journal / Writing Notes

freestyle
(yourstyle)

Weekly Calendar

WEEK MONTH YEAR

Cipher

writing time	editing time	social media	administration			

	SUNDAY	MONDAY	TUESDAY	WEDNESDAY	THURSDAY	FRIDAY	SATURDAY
Date							
7:00 – 8:00							
8:00 – 9:00							
9:00 – 10:00							
10:00 – 11:00							
11:00 – 12:00							
12:00 – 1:00							
1:00 – 2:00							
2:00 – 3:00							
3:00 – 4:00							
4:00 – 5:00							
5:00 – 6:00							
6:00 – 7:00							
7:00 – 8:00							
8:00 – 9:00							
9:00 – 10:00							
10:00 – 11:00							

Weekly Social Media Posts

MONDAY	PLATFORM: POSTS 1. 2. NOTES:	PLATFORM: POSTS 1. 2. NOTES:	PLATFORM: POSTS 1. 2. NOTES:
TUESDAY	PLATFORM: POSTS 1. 2. NOTES:	PLATFORM: POSTS 1. 2. NOTES:	PLATFORM: POSTS 1. 2. NOTES:
WEDNESDAY	PLATFORM: POSTS 1. 2. NOTES:	PLATFORM: POSTS 1. 2. NOTES:	PLATFORM: POSTS 1. 2. NOTES:
THURSDAY	PLATFORM: POSTS 1. 2. NOTES:	PLATFORM: POSTS 1. 2. NOTES:	PLATFORM: POSTS 1. 2. NOTES:
FRIDAY	PLATFORM: POSTS 1. 2. NOTES:	PLATFORM: POSTS 1. 2. NOTES:	PLATFORM: POSTS 1. 2. NOTES:

WEEKEND	SATURDAY	SUNDAY
	POSTS (PLATFORM) 1. 2. NOTES:	POSTS (PLATFORM) 1. 2. NOTES:

Weekly Journal / Writing Notes

freestyle
(yourstyle)

Month

Habit Tracker

	Write	Edit	Read	Post on Social Media	Scroll Through Media Feeds	Take Social Media Break	Marketing	Blog	Connected with Other Writers	Exercise	Get Outside	Self-care	Meditate							
1																				
2																				
3																				
4																				
5																				
6																				
7																				
8																				
9																				
10																				
11																				
12																				
13																				
14																				
15																				
16																				
17																				
18																				
19																				
20																				
21																				
22																				
23																				
24																				
25																				
26																				
27																				
28																				
29																				
30																				
31																				

Monthly Calendar

MONTH YEAR

SUNDAY	MONDAY	TUESDAY	WEDNESDAY	THURSDAY	FRIDAY	SATURDAY

To-Do List

MONTH: ____________________

ITEMS CARRIED OVER FROM PREVIOUS MONTH

- [ ] ______
- [ ] ______
- [ ] ______
- [ ] ______
- [ ] ______
- [ ] ______

TOP PRIORITY

- [ ] ______
- [ ] ______
- [ ] ______
- [ ] ______
- [ ] ______
- [ ] ______
- [ ] ______
- [ ] ______

IMPORTANT

- [ ] ______
- [ ] ______
- [ ] ______
- [ ] ______
- [ ] ______
- [ ] ______
- [ ] ______
- [ ] ______

TO DO

- [ ] ______
- [ ] ______
- [ ] ______
- [ ] ______
- [ ] ______
- [ ] ______
- [ ] ______
- [ ] ______
- [ ] ______
- [ ] ______
- [ ] ______
- [ ] ______
- [ ] ______
- [ ] ______
- [ ] ______
- [ ] ______
- [ ] ______
- [ ] ______
- [ ] ______
- [ ] ______
- [ ] ______
- [ ] ______
- [ ] ______
- [ ] ______

Serious writers write, inspired or not

WRITE

OVER TIME THEY DISCOVER THAT ROUTINE IS A BETTER FRIEND THAN inspiration

Month's Notes

Month's Blog Posts

1

2

3

4

5

Weekly Calendar

WEEK MONTH YEAR

Cipher

writing time	editing time	social media	administration			

	SUNDAY	MONDAY	TUESDAY	WEDNESDAY	THURSDAY	FRIDAY	SATURDAY
Date							
7:00 – 8:00							
8:00 – 9:00							
9:00 – 10:00							
10:00 – 11:00							
11:00 – 12:00							
12:00 – 1:00							
1:00 – 2:00							
2:00 – 3:00							
3:00 – 4:00							
4:00 – 5:00							
5:00 – 6:00							
6:00 – 7:00							
7:00 – 8:00							
8:00 – 9:00							
9:00 – 10:00							
10:00 – 11:00							

Weekly Social Media Posts

MONDAY	PLATFORM: POSTS 1. 2. NOTES:	PLATFORM: POSTS 1. 2. NOTES:	PLATFORM: POSTS 1. 2. NOTES:
TUESDAY	PLATFORM: POSTS 1. 2. NOTES:	PLATFORM: POSTS 1. 2. NOTES:	PLATFORM: POSTS 1. 2. NOTES:
WEDNESDAY	PLATFORM: POSTS 1. 2. NOTES:	PLATFORM: POSTS 1. 2. NOTES:	PLATFORM: POSTS 1. 2. NOTES:
THURSDAY	PLATFORM: POSTS 1. 2. NOTES:	PLATFORM: POSTS 1. 2. NOTES:	PLATFORM: POSTS 1. 2. NOTES:
FRIDAY	PLATFORM: POSTS 1. 2. NOTES:	PLATFORM: POSTS 1. 2. NOTES:	PLATFORM: POSTS 1. 2. NOTES:

WEEKEND	SATURDAY	SUNDAY
	POSTS (PLATFORM) 1. 2. NOTES:	POSTS (PLATFORM) 1. 2. NOTES:

Weekly Journal / Writing Notes

freestyle
(yourstyle)
LOVE
BROKEN

Weekly Calendar

WEEK MONTH YEAR

Cipher: writing time | editing time | social media | administration

Date	SUNDAY	MONDAY	TUESDAY	WEDNESDAY	THURSDAY	FRIDAY	SATURDAY
7:00 – 8:00							
8:00 – 9:00							
9:00 – 10:00							
10:00 – 11:00							
11:00 – 12:00							
12:00 – 1:00							
1:00 – 2:00							
2:00 – 3:00							
3:00 – 4:00							
4:00 – 5:00							
5:00 – 6:00							
6:00 – 7:00							
7:00 – 8:00							
8:00 – 9:00							
9:00 – 10:00							
10:00 – 11:00							

Weekly Social Media Posts

MONDAY	PLATFORM: POSTS 1. 2. NOTES:	PLATFORM: POSTS 1. 2. NOTES:	PLATFORM: POSTS 1. 2. NOTES:
TUESDAY	PLATFORM: POSTS 1. 2. NOTES:	PLATFORM: POSTS 1. 2. NOTES:	PLATFORM: POSTS 1. 2. NOTES:
WEDNESDAY	PLATFORM: POSTS 1. 2. NOTES:	PLATFORM: POSTS 1. 2. NOTES:	PLATFORM: POSTS 1. 2. NOTES:
THURSDAY	PLATFORM: POSTS 1. 2. NOTES:	PLATFORM: POSTS 1. 2. NOTES:	PLATFORM: POSTS 1. 2. NOTES:
FRIDAY	PLATFORM: POSTS 1. 2. NOTES:	PLATFORM: POSTS 1. 2. NOTES:	PLATFORM: POSTS 1. 2. NOTES:

WEEKEND	SATURDAY POSTS (PLATFORM) 1. 2. NOTES:	SUNDAY POSTS (PLATFORM) 1. 2. NOTES:

Weekly Journal / Writing Notes

freestyle
(yourstyle)

Weekly Calendar

WEEK MONTH YEAR

Cipher

writing time	editing time	social media	administration			

	SUNDAY	MONDAY	TUESDAY	WEDNESDAY	THURSDAY	FRIDAY	SATURDAY
Date							
7:00 – 8:00							
8:00 – 9:00							
9:00 – 10:00							
10:00 – 11:00							
11:00 – 12:00							
12:00 – 1:00							
1:00 – 2:00							
2:00 – 3:00							
3:00 – 4:00							
4:00 – 5:00							
5:00 – 6:00							
6:00 – 7:00							
7:00 – 8:00							
8:00 – 9:00							
9:00 – 10:00							
10:00 – 11:00							

Weekly Social Media Posts

MONDAY	PLATFORM: POSTS 1. 2. NOTES:	PLATFORM: POSTS 1. 2. NOTES:	PLATFORM: POSTS 1. 2. NOTES:
TUESDAY	PLATFORM: POSTS 1. 2. NOTES:	PLATFORM: POSTS 1. 2. NOTES:	PLATFORM: POSTS 1. 2. NOTES:
WEDNESDAY	PLATFORM: POSTS 1. 2. NOTES:	PLATFORM: POSTS 1. 2. NOTES:	PLATFORM: POSTS 1. 2. NOTES:
THURSDAY	PLATFORM: POSTS 1. 2. NOTES:	PLATFORM: POSTS 1. 2. NOTES:	PLATFORM: POSTS 1. 2. NOTES:
FRIDAY	PLATFORM: POSTS 1. 2. NOTES:	PLATFORM: POSTS 1. 2. NOTES:	PLATFORM: POSTS 1. 2. NOTES:

	SATURDAY	SUNDAY
WEEKEND	POSTS (PLATFORM) 1. 2. NOTES:	POSTS (PLATFORM) 1. 2. NOTES:

Weekly Journal / Writing Notes

freestyle
(yourstyle)

Weekly Calendar

WEEK MONTH YEAR

Cipher: writing time, editing time, social media, administration

	SUNDAY	MONDAY	TUESDAY	WEDNESDAY	THURSDAY	FRIDAY	SATURDAY
Date							
7:00 – 8:00							
8:00 – 9:00							
9:00 – 10:00							
10:00 – 11:00							
11:00 – 12:00							
12:00 – 1:00							
1:00 – 2:00							
2:00 – 3:00							
3:00 – 4:00							
4:00 – 5:00							
5:00 – 6:00							
6:00 – 7:00							
7:00 – 8:00							
8:00 – 9:00							
9:00 – 10:00							
10:00 – 11:00							

Weekly Social Media Posts

MONDAY	PLATFORM: POSTS 1. 2. NOTES:	PLATFORM: POSTS 1. 2. NOTES:	PLATFORM: POSTS 1. 2. NOTES:
TUESDAY	PLATFORM: POSTS 1. 2. NOTES:	PLATFORM: POSTS 1. 2. NOTES:	PLATFORM: POSTS 1. 2. NOTES:
WEDNESDAY	PLATFORM: POSTS 1. 2. NOTES:	PLATFORM: POSTS 1. 2. NOTES:	PLATFORM: POSTS 1. 2. NOTES:
THURSDAY	PLATFORM: POSTS 1. 2. NOTES:	PLATFORM: POSTS 1. 2. NOTES:	PLATFORM: POSTS 1. 2. NOTES:
FRIDAY	PLATFORM: POSTS 1. 2. NOTES:	PLATFORM: POSTS 1. 2. NOTES:	PLATFORM: POSTS 1. 2. NOTES:

WEEKEND	SATURDAY POSTS (PLATFORM) 1. 2. NOTES:	SUNDAY POSTS (PLATFORM) 1. 2. NOTES:

Weekly Journal / Writing Notes

freestyle
(yourstyle)

Weekly Calendar

WEEK MONTH YEAR

Cipher: writing time | editing time | social media | administration | | |

Date	SUNDAY	MONDAY	TUESDAY	WEDNESDAY	THURSDAY	FRIDAY	SATURDAY
7:00 – 8:00							
8:00 – 9:00							
9:00 – 10:00							
10:00 – 11:00							
11:00 – 12:00							
12:00 – 1:00							
1:00 – 2:00							
2:00 – 3:00							
3:00 – 4:00							
4:00 – 5:00							
5:00 – 6:00							
6:00 – 7:00							
7:00 – 8:00							
8:00 – 9:00							
9:00 – 10:00							
10:00 – 11:00							

Weekly Social Media Posts

MONDAY	PLATFORM: POSTS 1. 2. NOTES:	PLATFORM: POSTS 1. 2. NOTES:	PLATFORM: POSTS 1. 2. NOTES:
TUESDAY	PLATFORM: POSTS 1. 2. NOTES:	PLATFORM: POSTS 1. 2. NOTES:	PLATFORM: POSTS 1. 2. NOTES:
WEDNESDAY	PLATFORM: POSTS 1. 2. NOTES:	PLATFORM: POSTS 1. 2. NOTES:	PLATFORM: POSTS 1. 2. NOTES:
THURSDAY	PLATFORM: POSTS 1. 2. NOTES:	PLATFORM: POSTS 1. 2. NOTES:	PLATFORM: POSTS 1. 2. NOTES:
FRIDAY	PLATFORM: POSTS 1. 2. NOTES:	PLATFORM: POSTS 1. 2. NOTES:	PLATFORM: POSTS 1. 2. NOTES:

WEEKEND	SATURDAY	SUNDAY
	POSTS (PLATFORM) 1. 2. NOTES:	POSTS (PLATFORM) 1. 2. NOTES:

Weekly Journal / Writing Notes

freestyle
(yourstyle)

Month

Habit Tracker

	Write	Edit	Read	Post on Social Media	Scroll Through Media Feeds	Take Social Media Break	Marketing	Blog	Connected with Other Writers	Exercise	Get Outside	Self-care	Meditate							
1																				
2																				
3																				
4																				
5																				
6																				
7																				
8																				
9																				
10																				
11																				
12																				
13																				
14																				
15																				
16																				
17																				
18																				
19																				
20																				
21																				
22																				
23																				
24																				
25																				
26																				
27																				
28																				
29																				
30																				
31																				

Monthly Calendar

MONTH YEAR

SUNDAY	MONDAY	TUESDAY	WEDNESDAY	THURSDAY	FRIDAY	SATURDAY

To-Do List

MONTH: ______________________

ITEMS CARRIED OVER FROM PREVIOUS MONTH

- [ ] ____________________ - [ ] ____________________
- [ ] ____________________ - [ ] ____________________
- [ ] ____________________ - [ ] ____________________

TOP PRIORITY

- [ ] ____________________ - [ ] ____________________
- [ ] ____________________ - [ ] ____________________
- [ ] ____________________ - [ ] ____________________
- [ ] ____________________ - [ ] ____________________

IMPORTANT

- [ ] ____________________ - [ ] ____________________
- [ ] ____________________ - [ ] ____________________
- [ ] ____________________ - [ ] ____________________
- [ ] ____________________ - [ ] ____________________

TO DO

- [ ] ____________________ - [ ] ____________________
- [ ] ____________________ - [ ] ____________________
- [ ] ____________________ - [ ] ____________________
- [ ] ____________________ - [ ] ____________________
- [ ] ____________________ - [ ] ____________________
- [ ] ____________________ - [ ] ____________________
- [ ] ____________________ - [ ] ____________________
- [ ] ____________________ - [ ] ____________________
- [ ] ____________________ - [ ] ____________________
- [ ] ____________________ - [ ] ____________________
- [ ] ____________________ - [ ] ____________________
- [ ] ____________________ - [ ] ____________________

Month's Notes

Month's Blog Posts

1

2

3

4

5

Weekly Calendar

WEEK MONTH YEAR

Cipher

writing time | editing time | social media | administration

Date	SUNDAY	MONDAY	TUESDAY	WEDNESDAY	THURSDAY	FRIDAY	SATURDAY
7:00 – 8:00							
8:00 – 9:00							
9:00 – 10:00							
10:00 – 11:00							
11:00 – 12:00							
12:00 – 1:00							
1:00 – 2:00							
2:00 – 3:00							
3:00 – 4:00							
4:00 – 5:00							
5:00 – 6:00							
6:00 – 7:00							
7:00 – 8:00							
8:00 – 9:00							
9:00 – 10:00							
10:00 – 11:00							

Weekly Social Media Posts

MONDAY	PLATFORM: POSTS 1. 2. NOTES:	PLATFORM: POSTS 1. 2. NOTES:	PLATFORM: POSTS 1. 2. NOTES:
TUESDAY	PLATFORM: POSTS 1. 2. NOTES:	PLATFORM: POSTS 1. 2. NOTES:	PLATFORM: POSTS 1. 2. NOTES:
WEDNESDAY	PLATFORM: POSTS 1. 2. NOTES:	PLATFORM: POSTS 1. 2. NOTES:	PLATFORM: POSTS 1. 2. NOTES:
THURSDAY	PLATFORM: POSTS 1. 2. NOTES:	PLATFORM: POSTS 1. 2. NOTES:	PLATFORM: POSTS 1. 2. NOTES:
FRIDAY	PLATFORM: POSTS 1. 2. NOTES:	PLATFORM: POSTS 1. 2. NOTES:	PLATFORM: POSTS 1. 2. NOTES:

WEEKEND	SATURDAY	SUNDAY
	POSTS (PLATFORM) 1. 2. NOTES:	POSTS (PLATFORM) 1. 2. NOTES:

Weekly Journal / Writing Notes

freestyle
(yourstyle)
LOVE
BROKEN

Weekly Calendar

WEEK MONTH YEAR

Cipher

writing time	editing time	social media	administration			

	SUNDAY	MONDAY	TUESDAY	WEDNESDAY	THURSDAY	FRIDAY	SATURDAY
Date							
7:00 – 8:00							
8:00 – 9:00							
9:00 – 10:00							
10:00 – 11:00							
11:00 – 12:00							
12:00 – 1:00							
1:00 – 2:00							
2:00 – 3:00							
3:00 – 4:00							
4:00 – 5:00							
5:00 – 6:00							
6:00 – 7:00							
7:00 – 8:00							
8:00 – 9:00							
9:00 – 10:00							
10:00 – 11:00							

Weekly Social Media Posts

MONDAY	PLATFORM: POSTS 1. 2. NOTES:	PLATFORM: POSTS 1. 2. NOTES:	PLATFORM: POSTS 1. 2. NOTES:
TUESDAY	PLATFORM: POSTS 1. 2. NOTES:	PLATFORM: POSTS 1. 2. NOTES:	PLATFORM: POSTS 1. 2. NOTES:
WEDNESDAY	PLATFORM: POSTS 1. 2. NOTES:	PLATFORM: POSTS 1. 2. NOTES:	PLATFORM: POSTS 1. 2. NOTES:
THURSDAY	PLATFORM: POSTS 1. 2. NOTES:	PLATFORM: POSTS 1. 2. NOTES:	PLATFORM: POSTS 1. 2. NOTES:
FRIDAY	PLATFORM: POSTS 1. 2. NOTES:	PLATFORM: POSTS 1. 2. NOTES:	PLATFORM: POSTS 1. 2. NOTES:

WEEKEND	SATURDAY	SUNDAY
	POSTS (PLATFORM) 1. 2. NOTES:	POSTS (PLATFORM) 1. 2. NOTES:

Weekly Journal / Writing Notes

freestyle
(yourstyle)

Weekly Calendar

WEEK MONTH YEAR

Cipher: writing time | editing time | social media | administration

Date	SUNDAY	MONDAY	TUESDAY	WEDNESDAY	THURSDAY	FRIDAY	SATURDAY
7:00 – 8:00							
8:00 – 9:00							
9:00 – 10:00							
10:00 – 11:00							
11:00 – 12:00							
12:00 – 1:00							
1:00 – 2:00							
2:00 – 3:00							
3:00 – 4:00							
4:00 – 5:00							
5:00 – 6:00							
6:00 – 7:00							
7:00 – 8:00							
8:00 – 9:00							
9:00 – 10:00							
10:00 – 11:00							

Weekly Social Media Posts

MONDAY	PLATFORM: POSTS 1. 2. NOTES:	PLATFORM: POSTS 1. 2. NOTES:	PLATFORM: POSTS 1. 2. NOTES:
TUESDAY	PLATFORM: POSTS 1. 2. NOTES:	PLATFORM: POSTS 1. 2. NOTES:	PLATFORM: POSTS 1. 2. NOTES:
WEDNESDAY	PLATFORM: POSTS 1. 2. NOTES:	PLATFORM: POSTS 1. 2. NOTES:	PLATFORM: POSTS 1. 2. NOTES:
THURSDAY	PLATFORM: POSTS 1. 2. NOTES:	PLATFORM: POSTS 1. 2. NOTES:	PLATFORM: POSTS 1. 2. NOTES:
FRIDAY	PLATFORM: POSTS 1. 2. NOTES:	PLATFORM: POSTS 1. 2. NOTES:	PLATFORM: POSTS 1. 2. NOTES:

WEEKEND	SATURDAY	SUNDAY
	POSTS (PLATFORM) 1. 2. NOTES:	POSTS (PLATFORM) 1. 2. NOTES:

Weekly Journal / Writing Notes

freestyle
(yourstyle)

Weekly Calendar

WEEK MONTH YEAR

Cipher

writing time	editing time	social media	administration			

Date	SUNDAY	MONDAY	TUESDAY	WEDNESDAY	THURSDAY	FRIDAY	SATURDAY
7:00 – 8:00							
8:00 – 9:00							
9:00 – 10:00							
10:00 – 11:00							
11:00 – 12:00							
12:00 – 1:00							
1:00 – 2:00							
2:00 – 3:00							
3:00 – 4:00							
4:00 – 5:00							
5:00 – 6:00							
6:00 – 7:00							
7:00 – 8:00							
8:00 – 9:00							
9:00 – 10:00							
10:00 – 11:00							

Weekly Social Media Posts

MONDAY	PLATFORM: POSTS 1. 2. NOTES:	PLATFORM: POSTS 1. 2. NOTES:	PLATFORM: POSTS 1. 2. NOTES:
TUESDAY	PLATFORM: POSTS 1. 2. NOTES:	PLATFORM: POSTS 1. 2. NOTES:	PLATFORM: POSTS 1. 2. NOTES:
WEDNESDAY	PLATFORM: POSTS 1. 2. NOTES:	PLATFORM: POSTS 1. 2. NOTES:	PLATFORM: POSTS 1. 2. NOTES:
THURSDAY	PLATFORM: POSTS 1. 2. NOTES:	PLATFORM: POSTS 1. 2. NOTES:	PLATFORM: POSTS 1. 2. NOTES:
FRIDAY	PLATFORM: POSTS 1. 2. NOTES:	PLATFORM: POSTS 1. 2. NOTES:	PLATFORM: POSTS 1. 2. NOTES:

WEEKEND	SATURDAY	SUNDAY
	POSTS (PLATFORM) 1. 2. NOTES:	POSTS (PLATFORM) 1. 2. NOTES:

Weekly Journal / Writing Notes

freestyle
(yourstyle)

Weekly Calendar

WEEK MONTH YEAR

Cipher: writing time, editing time, social media, administration

Date	SUNDAY	MONDAY	TUESDAY	WEDNESDAY	THURSDAY	FRIDAY	SATURDAY
7:00 – 8:00							
8:00 – 9:00							
9:00 – 10:00							
10:00 – 11:00							
11:00 – 12:00							
12:00 – 1:00							
1:00 – 2:00							
2:00 – 3:00							
3:00 – 4:00							
4:00 – 5:00							
5:00 – 6:00							
6:00 – 7:00							
7:00 – 8:00							
8:00 – 9:00							
9:00 – 10:00							
10:00 – 11:00							

Weekly Social Media Posts

Day			
MONDAY	PLATFORM: POSTS 1. 2. NOTES:	PLATFORM: POSTS 1. 2. NOTES:	PLATFORM: POSTS 1. 2. NOTES:
TUESDAY	PLATFORM: POSTS 1. 2. NOTES:	PLATFORM: POSTS 1. 2. NOTES:	PLATFORM: POSTS 1. 2. NOTES:
WEDNESDAY	PLATFORM: POSTS 1. 2. NOTES:	PLATFORM: POSTS 1. 2. NOTES:	PLATFORM: POSTS 1. 2. NOTES:
THURSDAY	PLATFORM: POSTS 1. 2. NOTES:	PLATFORM: POSTS 1. 2. NOTES:	PLATFORM: POSTS 1. 2. NOTES:
FRIDAY	PLATFORM: POSTS 1. 2. NOTES:	PLATFORM: POSTS 1. 2. NOTES:	PLATFORM: POSTS 1. 2. NOTES:

WEEKEND	SATURDAY	SUNDAY
	POSTS (PLATFORM) 1. 2. NOTES:	POSTS (PLATFORM) 1. 2. NOTES:

Weekly Journal / Writing Notes

freestyle
(yourstyle)

Month

Habit Tracker

	Write	Edit	Read	Post on Social Media	Scroll Through Media Feeds	Take Social Media Break	Marketing	Blog	Connected with Other Writers	Exercise	Get Outside	Self-care	Meditate							
1																				
2																				
3																				
4																				
5																				
6																				
7																				
8																				
9																				
10																				
11																				
12																				
13																				
14																				
15																				
16																				
17																				
18																				
19																				
20																				
21																				
22																				
23																				
24																				
25																				
26																				
27																				
28																				
29																				
30																				
31																				

Monthly Calendar

MONTH YEAR

SUNDAY	MONDAY	TUESDAY	WEDNESDAY	THURSDAY	FRIDAY	SATURDAY

To-Do List

MONTH: ______________________

ITEMS CARRIED OVER FROM PREVIOUS MONTH

- [ ]
- [ ]
- [ ]
- [ ]
- [ ]
- [ ]

TOP PRIORITY

- [ ]
- [ ]
- [ ]
- [ ]
- [ ]
- [ ]
- [ ]
- [ ]

IMPORTANT

- [ ]
- [ ]
- [ ]
- [ ]
- [ ]
- [ ]
- [ ]
- [ ]

TO DO

- [ ]
- [ ]
- [ ]
- [ ]
- [ ]
- [ ]
- [ ]
- [ ]
- [ ]
- [ ]
- [ ]
- [ ]
- [ ]
- [ ]
- [ ]
- [ ]
- [ ]
- [ ]
- [ ]
- [ ]
- [ ]
- [ ]
- [ ]
- [ ]

Month's Notes

Month's Blog Posts

1

2

3

4

5

Weekly Calendar

WEEK MONTH YEAR

Cipher

writing time	editing time	social media	administration			

	SUNDAY	MONDAY	TUESDAY	WEDNESDAY	THURSDAY	FRIDAY	SATURDAY
Date							
7:00 – 8:00							
8:00 – 9:00							
9:00 – 10:00							
10:00 – 11:00							
11:00 – 12:00							
12:00 – 1:00							
1:00 – 2:00							
2:00 – 3:00							
3:00 – 4:00							
4:00 – 5:00							
5:00 – 6:00							
6:00 – 7:00							
7:00 – 8:00							
8:00 – 9:00							
9:00 – 10:00							
10:00 – 11:00							

Weekly Social Media Posts

MONDAY	PLATFORM: POSTS 1. 2. NOTES:	PLATFORM: POSTS 1. 2. NOTES:	PLATFORM: POSTS 1. 2. NOTES:
TUESDAY	PLATFORM: POSTS 1. 2. NOTES:	PLATFORM: POSTS 1. 2. NOTES:	PLATFORM: POSTS 1. 2. NOTES:
WEDNESDAY	PLATFORM: POSTS 1. 2. NOTES:	PLATFORM: POSTS 1. 2. NOTES:	PLATFORM: POSTS 1. 2. NOTES:
THURSDAY	PLATFORM: POSTS 1. 2. NOTES:	PLATFORM: POSTS 1. 2. NOTES:	PLATFORM: POSTS 1. 2. NOTES:
FRIDAY	PLATFORM: POSTS 1. 2. NOTES:	PLATFORM: POSTS 1. 2. NOTES:	PLATFORM: POSTS 1. 2. NOTES:

WEEKEND	SATURDAY	SUNDAY
	POSTS (PLATFORM) 1. 2. NOTES:	POSTS (PLATFORM) 1. 2. NOTES:

Weekly Journal / Writing Notes

freestyle
(yourstyle)
LOVE
BROKEN

Weekly Calendar

WEEK MONTH YEAR

Cipher: writing time | editing time | social media | administration

	SUNDAY	MONDAY	TUESDAY	WEDNESDAY	THURSDAY	FRIDAY	SATURDAY
Date							
7:00 – 8:00							
8:00 – 9:00							
9:00 – 10:00							
10:00 – 11:00							
11:00 – 12:00							
12:00 – 1:00							
1:00 – 2:00							
2:00 – 3:00							
3:00 – 4:00							
4:00 – 5:00							
5:00 – 6:00							
6:00 – 7:00							
7:00 – 8:00							
8:00 – 9:00							
9:00 – 10:00							
10:00 – 11:00							

Weekly Social Media Posts

MONDAY	PLATFORM: POSTS 1. 2. NOTES:	PLATFORM: POSTS 1. 2. NOTES:	PLATFORM: POSTS 1. 2. NOTES:
TUESDAY	PLATFORM: POSTS 1. 2. NOTES:	PLATFORM: POSTS 1. 2. NOTES:	PLATFORM: POSTS 1. 2. NOTES:
WEDNESDAY	PLATFORM: POSTS 1. 2. NOTES:	PLATFORM: POSTS 1. 2. NOTES:	PLATFORM: POSTS 1. 2. NOTES:
THURSDAY	PLATFORM: POSTS 1. 2. NOTES:	PLATFORM: POSTS 1. 2. NOTES:	PLATFORM: POSTS 1. 2. NOTES:
FRIDAY	PLATFORM: POSTS 1. 2. NOTES:	PLATFORM: POSTS 1. 2. NOTES:	PLATFORM: POSTS 1. 2. NOTES:

WEEKEND	SATURDAY POSTS (PLATFORM) 1. 2. NOTES:	SUNDAY POSTS (PLATFORM) 1. 2. NOTES:

Weekly Journal / Writing Notes

freestyle
(yourstyle)

Weekly Calendar

WEEK MONTH YEAR

Cipher

writing time	editing time	social media	administration			

	SUNDAY	MONDAY	TUESDAY	WEDNESDAY	THURSDAY	FRIDAY	SATURDAY
Date							
7:00 – 8:00							
8:00 – 9:00							
9:00 – 10:00							
10:00 – 11:00							
11:00 – 12:00							
12:00 – 1:00							
1:00 – 2:00							
2:00 – 3:00							
3:00 – 4:00							
4:00 – 5:00							
5:00 – 6:00							
6:00 – 7:00							
7:00 – 8:00							
8:00 – 9:00							
9:00 – 10:00							
10:00 – 11:00							

Weekly Social Media Posts

MONDAY	PLATFORM: POSTS 1. 2. NOTES:	PLATFORM: POSTS 1. 2. NOTES:	PLATFORM: POSTS 1. 2. NOTES:
TUESDAY	PLATFORM: POSTS 1. 2. NOTES:	PLATFORM: POSTS 1. 2. NOTES:	PLATFORM: POSTS 1. 2. NOTES:
WEDNESDAY	PLATFORM: POSTS 1. 2. NOTES:	PLATFORM: POSTS 1. 2. NOTES:	PLATFORM: POSTS 1. 2. NOTES:
THURSDAY	PLATFORM: POSTS 1. 2. NOTES:	PLATFORM: POSTS 1. 2. NOTES:	PLATFORM: POSTS 1. 2. NOTES:
FRIDAY	PLATFORM: POSTS 1. 2. NOTES:	PLATFORM: POSTS 1. 2. NOTES:	PLATFORM: POSTS 1. 2. NOTES:

WEEKEND	SATURDAY	SUNDAY
	POSTS (PLATFORM) 1. 2. NOTES:	POSTS (PLATFORM) 1. 2. NOTES:

Weekly Journal / Writing Notes

freestyle
(yourstyle)

Weekly Calendar

WEEK MONTH YEAR

Cipher: writing time | editing time | social media | administration | | |

	SUNDAY	MONDAY	TUESDAY	WEDNESDAY	THURSDAY	FRIDAY	SATURDAY
Date							
7:00 – 8:00							
8:00 – 9:00							
9:00 – 10:00							
10:00 – 11:00							
11:00 – 12:00							
12:00 – 1:00							
1:00 – 2:00							
2:00 – 3:00							
3:00 – 4:00							
4:00 – 5:00							
5:00 – 6:00							
6:00 – 7:00							
7:00 – 8:00							
8:00 – 9:00							
9:00 – 10:00							
10:00 – 11:00							

Weekly Social Media Posts

MONDAY	PLATFORM: POSTS 1. 2. NOTES:	PLATFORM: POSTS 1. 2. NOTES:	PLATFORM: POSTS 1. 2. NOTES:
TUESDAY	PLATFORM: POSTS 1. 2. NOTES:	PLATFORM: POSTS 1. 2. NOTES:	PLATFORM: POSTS 1. 2. NOTES:
WEDNESDAY	PLATFORM: POSTS 1. 2. NOTES:	PLATFORM: POSTS 1. 2. NOTES:	PLATFORM: POSTS 1. 2. NOTES:
THURSDAY	PLATFORM: POSTS 1. 2. NOTES:	PLATFORM: POSTS 1. 2. NOTES:	PLATFORM: POSTS 1. 2. NOTES:
FRIDAY	PLATFORM: POSTS 1. 2. NOTES:	PLATFORM: POSTS 1. 2. NOTES:	PLATFORM: POSTS 1. 2. NOTES:

WEEKEND	SATURDAY	SUNDAY
	POSTS (PLATFORM) 1. 2. NOTES:	POSTS (PLATFORM) 1. 2. NOTES:

Weekly Journal / Writing Notes

freestyle
(yourstyle)

Weekly Calendar

WEEK MONTH YEAR

Cipher: writing time | editing time | social media | administration

	SUNDAY	MONDAY	TUESDAY	WEDNESDAY	THURSDAY	FRIDAY	SATURDAY
Date							
7:00 – 8:00							
8:00 – 9:00							
9:00 – 10:00							
10:00 – 11:00							
11:00 – 12:00							
12:00 – 1:00							
1:00 – 2:00							
2:00 – 3:00							
3:00 – 4:00							
4:00 – 5:00							
5:00 – 6:00							
6:00 – 7:00							
7:00 – 8:00							
8:00 – 9:00							
9:00 – 10:00							
10:00 – 11:00							

Weekly Social Media Posts

MONDAY	PLATFORM: POSTS 1. 2. NOTES:	PLATFORM: POSTS 1. 2. NOTES:	PLATFORM: POSTS 1. 2. NOTES:
TUESDAY	PLATFORM: POSTS 1. 2. NOTES:	PLATFORM: POSTS 1. 2. NOTES:	PLATFORM: POSTS 1. 2. NOTES:
WEDNESDAY	PLATFORM: POSTS 1. 2. NOTES:	PLATFORM: POSTS 1. 2. NOTES:	PLATFORM: POSTS 1. 2. NOTES:
THURSDAY	PLATFORM: POSTS 1. 2. NOTES:	PLATFORM: POSTS 1. 2. NOTES:	PLATFORM: POSTS 1. 2. NOTES:
FRIDAY	PLATFORM: POSTS 1. 2. NOTES:	PLATFORM: POSTS 1. 2. NOTES:	PLATFORM: POSTS 1. 2. NOTES:

	SATURDAY	SUNDAY
WEEKEND	POSTS (PLATFORM) 1. 2. NOTES:	POSTS (PLATFORM) 1. 2. NOTES:

Weekly Journal / Writing Notes

freestyle
(yourstyle)

Month

Habit Tracker

	Write	Edit	Read	Post on Social Media	Scroll Through Media Feeds	Take Social Media Break	Marketing	Blog	Connected with Other Writers	Exercise	Get Outside	Self-care	Meditate							
1																				
2																				
3																				
4																				
5																				
6																				
7																				
8																				
9																				
10																				
11																				
12																				
13																				
14																				
15																				
16																				
17																				
18																				
19																				
20																				
21																				
22																				
23																				
24																				
25																				
26																				
27																				
28																				
29																				
30																				
31																				

Monthly Calendar

MONTH YEAR

SUNDAY	MONDAY	TUESDAY	WEDNESDAY	THURSDAY	FRIDAY	SATURDAY

To-Do List

MONTH: ____________________

ITEMS CARRIED OVER FROM PREVIOUS MONTH

- [ ] ____________________
- [ ] ____________________
- [ ] ____________________
- [ ] ____________________
- [ ] ____________________
- [ ] ____________________

TOP PRIORITY

- [ ] ____________________
- [ ] ____________________
- [ ] ____________________
- [ ] ____________________
- [ ] ____________________
- [ ] ____________________
- [ ] ____________________
- [ ] ____________________

IMPORTANT

- [ ] ____________________
- [ ] ____________________
- [ ] ____________________
- [ ] ____________________
- [ ] ____________________
- [ ] ____________________
- [ ] ____________________
- [ ] ____________________

TO DO

- [ ] ____________________
- [ ] ____________________
- [ ] ____________________
- [ ] ____________________
- [ ] ____________________
- [ ] ____________________
- [ ] ____________________
- [ ] ____________________
- [ ] ____________________
- [ ] ____________________
- [ ] ____________________
- [ ] ____________________
- [ ] ____________________
- [ ] ____________________
- [ ] ____________________
- [ ] ____________________
- [ ] ____________________
- [ ] ____________________
- [ ] ____________________
- [ ] ____________________
- [ ] ____________________
- [ ] ____________________
- [ ] ____________________
- [ ] ____________________

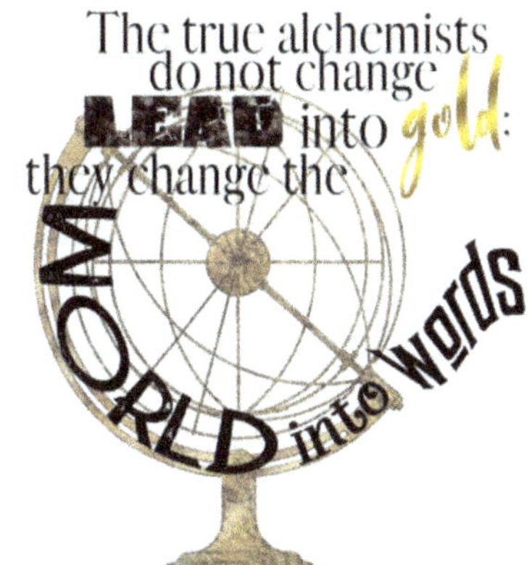

Month's Notes

Month's Blog Posts

1

2

3

4

5

Weekly Calendar

WEEK MONTH YEAR

Cipher

writing time	editing time	social media	administration			

	SUNDAY	MONDAY	TUESDAY	WEDNESDAY	THURSDAY	FRIDAY	SATURDAY
Date							
7:00 – 8:00							
8:00 – 9:00							
9:00 – 10:00							
10:00 – 11:00							
11:00 – 12:00							
12:00 – 1:00							
1:00 – 2:00							
2:00 – 3:00							
3:00 – 4:00							
4:00 – 5:00							
5:00 – 6:00							
6:00 – 7:00							
7:00 – 8:00							
8:00 – 9:00							
9:00 – 10:00							
10:00 – 11:00							

Weekly Social Media Posts

MONDAY	PLATFORM: POSTS 1. 2. NOTES:	PLATFORM: POSTS 1. 2. NOTES:	PLATFORM: POSTS 1. 2. NOTES:
TUESDAY	PLATFORM: POSTS 1. 2. NOTES:	PLATFORM: POSTS 1. 2. NOTES:	PLATFORM: POSTS 1. 2. NOTES:
WEDNESDAY	PLATFORM: POSTS 1. 2. NOTES:	PLATFORM: POSTS 1. 2. NOTES:	PLATFORM: POSTS 1. 2. NOTES:
THURSDAY	PLATFORM: POSTS 1. 2. NOTES:	PLATFORM: POSTS 1. 2. NOTES:	PLATFORM: POSTS 1. 2. NOTES:
FRIDAY	PLATFORM: POSTS 1. 2. NOTES:	PLATFORM: POSTS 1. 2. NOTES:	PLATFORM: POSTS 1. 2. NOTES:

WEEKEND	SATURDAY	SUNDAY
	POSTS (PLATFORM) 1. 2. NOTES:	POSTS (PLATFORM) 1. 2. NOTES:

Weekly Journal / Writing Notes

freestyle
(yourstyle)
LOVE
BROKEN

Weekly Calendar

WEEK MONTH YEAR

Cipher: writing time, editing time, social media, administration

	SUNDAY	MONDAY	TUESDAY	WEDNESDAY	THURSDAY	FRIDAY	SATURDAY
Date							
7:00 – 8:00							
8:00 – 9:00							
9:00 – 10:00							
10:00 – 11:00							
11:00 – 12:00							
12:00 – 1:00							
1:00 – 2:00							
2:00 – 3:00							
3:00 – 4:00							
4:00 – 5:00							
5:00 – 6:00							
6:00 – 7:00							
7:00 – 8:00							
8:00 – 9:00							
9:00 – 10:00							
10:00 – 11:00							

Weekly Social Media Posts

MONDAY	PLATFORM: POSTS 1. 2. NOTES:	PLATFORM: POSTS 1. 2. NOTES:	PLATFORM: POSTS 1. 2. NOTES:
TUESDAY	PLATFORM: POSTS 1. 2. NOTES:	PLATFORM: POSTS 1. 2. NOTES:	PLATFORM: POSTS 1. 2. NOTES:
WEDNESDAY	PLATFORM: POSTS 1. 2. NOTES:	PLATFORM: POSTS 1. 2. NOTES:	PLATFORM: POSTS 1. 2. NOTES:
THURSDAY	PLATFORM: POSTS 1. 2. NOTES:	PLATFORM: POSTS 1. 2. NOTES:	PLATFORM: POSTS 1. 2. NOTES:
FRIDAY	PLATFORM: POSTS 1. 2. NOTES:	PLATFORM: POSTS 1. 2. NOTES:	PLATFORM: POSTS 1. 2. NOTES:

WEEKEND	SATURDAY	SUNDAY
	POSTS (PLATFORM) 1. 2. NOTES:	POSTS (PLATFORM) 1. 2. NOTES:

Weekly Journal / Writing Notes

freestyle
(yourstyle)

Weekly Calendar

WEEK MONTH YEAR

Cipher: writing time | editing time | social media | administration | ____ | ____ | ____

	SUNDAY	MONDAY	TUESDAY	WEDNESDAY	THURSDAY	FRIDAY	SATURDAY
Date							
7:00 – 8:00							
8:00 – 9:00							
9:00 – 10:00							
10:00 – 11:00							
11:00 – 12:00							
12:00 – 1:00							
1:00 – 2:00							
2:00 – 3:00							
3:00 – 4:00							
4:00 – 5:00							
5:00 – 6:00							
6:00 – 7:00							
7:00 – 8:00							
8:00 – 9:00							
9:00 – 10:00							
10:00 – 11:00							

Weekly Social Media Posts

MONDAY	PLATFORM: POSTS 1. 2. NOTES:	PLATFORM: POSTS 1. 2. NOTES:	PLATFORM: POSTS 1. 2. NOTES:
TUESDAY	PLATFORM: POSTS 1. 2. NOTES:	PLATFORM: POSTS 1. 2. NOTES:	PLATFORM: POSTS 1. 2. NOTES:
WEDNESDAY	PLATFORM: POSTS 1. 2. NOTES:	PLATFORM: POSTS 1. 2. NOTES:	PLATFORM: POSTS 1. 2. NOTES:
THURSDAY	PLATFORM: POSTS 1. 2. NOTES:	PLATFORM: POSTS 1. 2. NOTES:	PLATFORM: POSTS 1. 2. NOTES:
FRIDAY	PLATFORM: POSTS 1. 2. NOTES:	PLATFORM: POSTS 1. 2. NOTES:	PLATFORM: POSTS 1. 2. NOTES:

WEEKEND	SATURDAY POSTS (PLATFORM) 1. 2. NOTES:	SUNDAY POSTS (PLATFORM) 1. 2. NOTES:

Weekly Journal / Writing Notes

freestyle
(yourstyle)

Weekly Calendar

WEEK MONTH YEAR

Cipher: writing time | editing time | social media | administration | ____ | ____ | ____

	SUNDAY	MONDAY	TUESDAY	WEDNESDAY	THURSDAY	FRIDAY	SATURDAY
Date							
7:00 – 8:00							
8:00 – 9:00							
9:00 – 10:00							
10:00 – 11:00							
11:00 – 12:00							
12:00 – 1:00							
1:00 – 2:00							
2:00 – 3:00							
3:00 – 4:00							
4:00 – 5:00							
5:00 – 6:00							
6:00 – 7:00							
7:00 – 8:00							
8:00 – 9:00							
9:00 – 10:00							
10:00 – 11:00							

Weekly Social Media Posts

MONDAY	PLATFORM: POSTS 1. 2. NOTES:	PLATFORM: POSTS 1. 2. NOTES:	PLATFORM: POSTS 1. 2. NOTES:
TUESDAY	PLATFORM: POSTS 1. 2. NOTES:	PLATFORM: POSTS 1. 2. NOTES:	PLATFORM: POSTS 1. 2. NOTES:
WEDNESDAY	PLATFORM: POSTS 1. 2. NOTES:	PLATFORM: POSTS 1. 2. NOTES:	PLATFORM: POSTS 1. 2. NOTES:
THURSDAY	PLATFORM: POSTS 1. 2. NOTES:	PLATFORM: POSTS 1. 2. NOTES:	PLATFORM: POSTS 1. 2. NOTES:
FRIDAY	PLATFORM: POSTS 1. 2. NOTES:	PLATFORM: POSTS 1. 2. NOTES:	PLATFORM: POSTS 1. 2. NOTES:

WEEKEND	SATURDAY	SUNDAY
	POSTS (PLATFORM) 1. 2. NOTES:	POSTS (PLATFORM) 1. 2. NOTES:

Weekly Journal / Writing Notes

freestyle
(yourstyle)

Weekly Calendar

WEEK MONTH YEAR

Cipher

writing time | editing time | social media | administration

Date	SUNDAY	MONDAY	TUESDAY	WEDNESDAY	THURSDAY	FRIDAY	SATURDAY
7:00 – 8:00							
8:00 – 9:00							
9:00 – 10:00							
10:00 – 11:00							
11:00 – 12:00							
12:00 – 1:00							
1:00 – 2:00							
2:00 – 3:00							
3:00 – 4:00							
4:00 – 5:00							
5:00 – 6:00							
6:00 – 7:00							
7:00 – 8:00							
8:00 – 9:00							
9:00 – 10:00							
10:00 – 11:00							

Weekly Social Media Posts

MONDAY	PLATFORM: POSTS 1. 2. NOTES:	PLATFORM: POSTS 1. 2. NOTES:	PLATFORM: POSTS 1. 2. NOTES:
TUESDAY	PLATFORM: POSTS 1. 2. NOTES:	PLATFORM: POSTS 1. 2. NOTES:	PLATFORM: POSTS 1. 2. NOTES:
WEDNESDAY	PLATFORM: POSTS 1. 2. NOTES:	PLATFORM: POSTS 1. 2. NOTES:	PLATFORM: POSTS 1. 2. NOTES:
THURSDAY	PLATFORM: POSTS 1. 2. NOTES:	PLATFORM: POSTS 1. 2. NOTES:	PLATFORM: POSTS 1. 2. NOTES:
FRIDAY	PLATFORM: POSTS 1. 2. NOTES:	PLATFORM: POSTS 1. 2. NOTES:	PLATFORM: POSTS 1. 2. NOTES:

WEEKEND	SATURDAY POSTS (PLATFORM) 1. 2. NOTES:	SUNDAY POSTS (PLATFORM) 1. 2. NOTES:

Weekly Journal / Writing Notes

freestyle
(yourstyle)

About the Author

CM Fick is experienced with both graphic design and web design. She is proficient in all aspects of the design process, and is accomplished with design principles, color theory, and art theory. She is also an unagented writer as of the publication of this book, but she aspires to traditionally publish her fiction works one day.

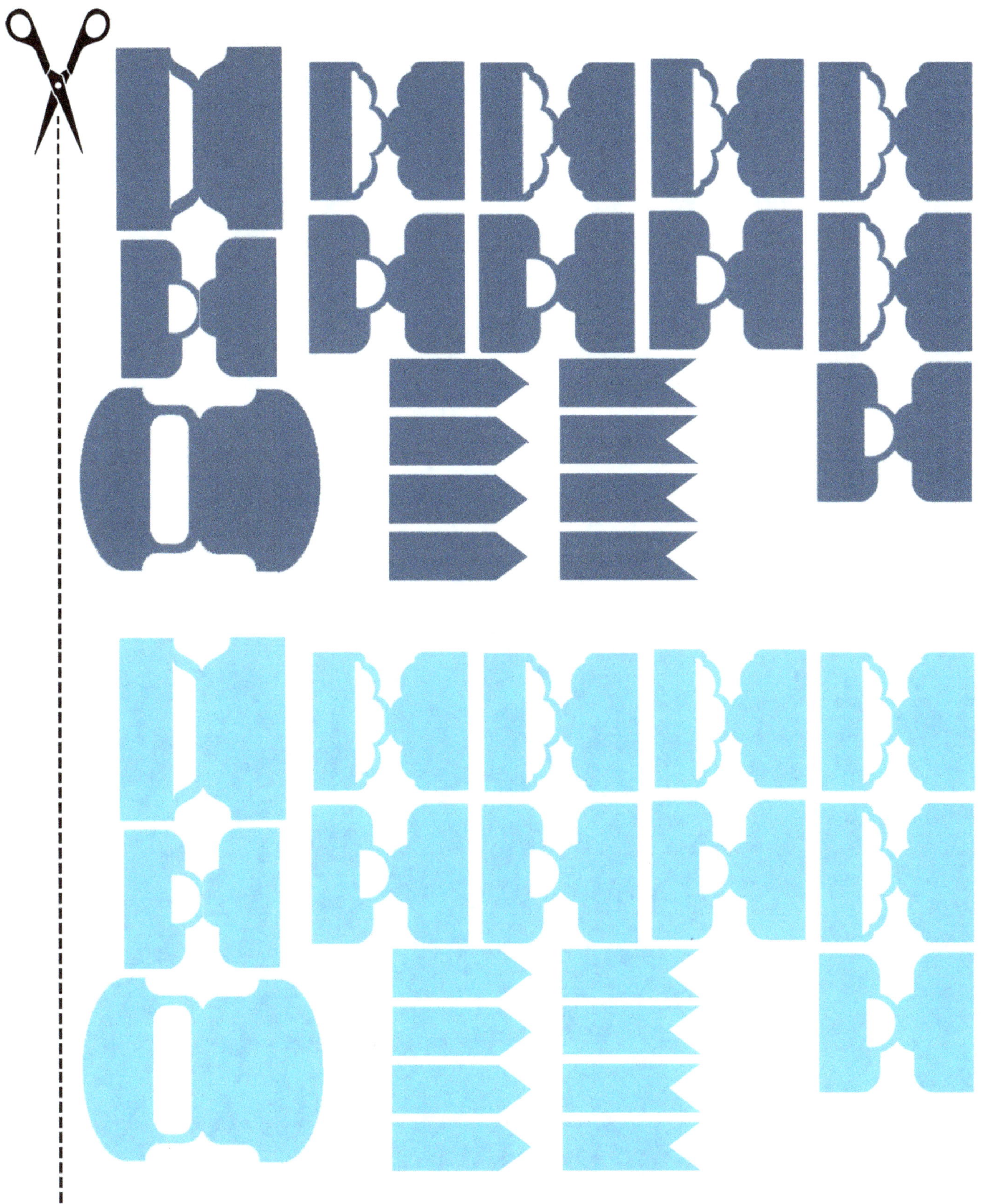

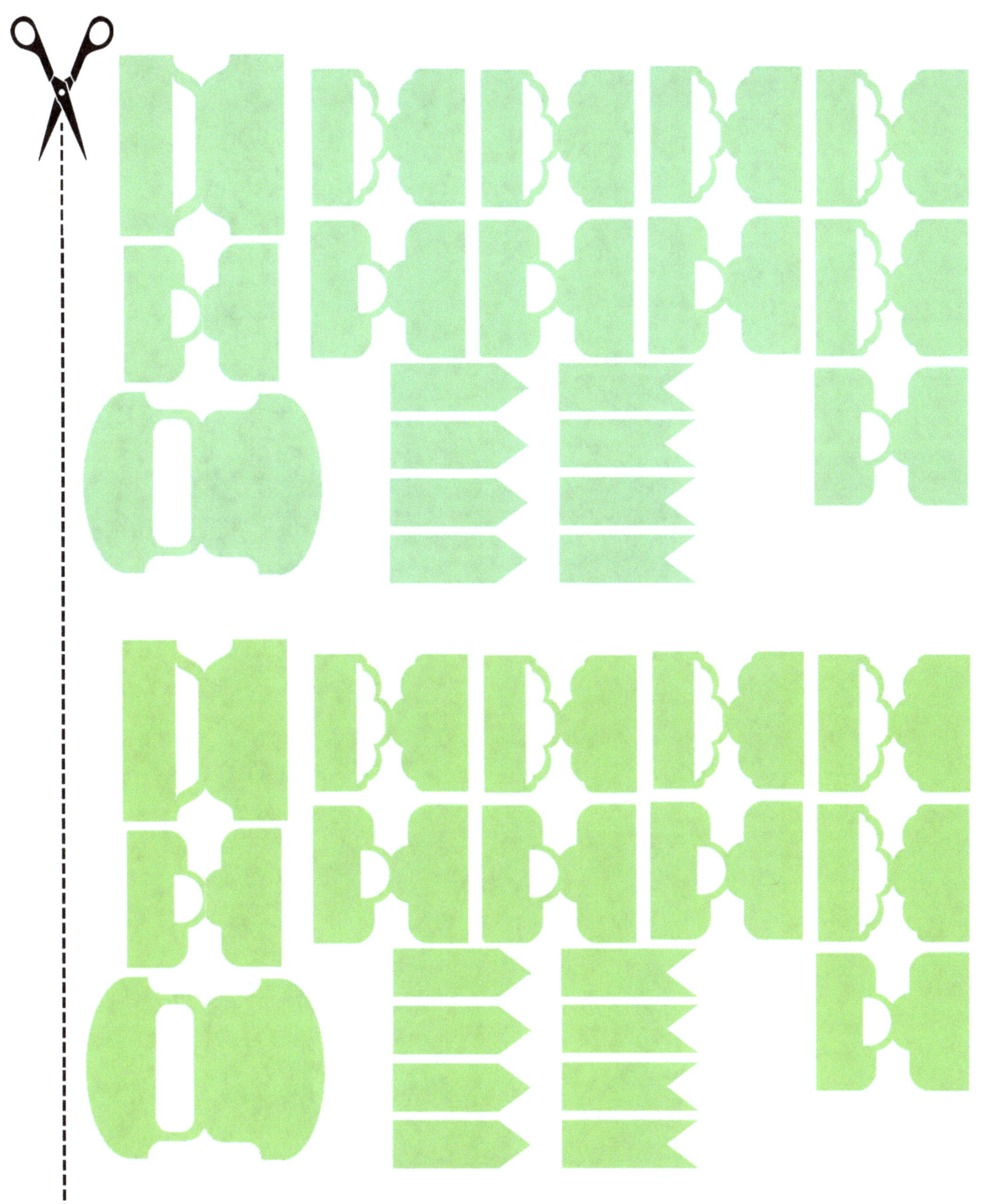

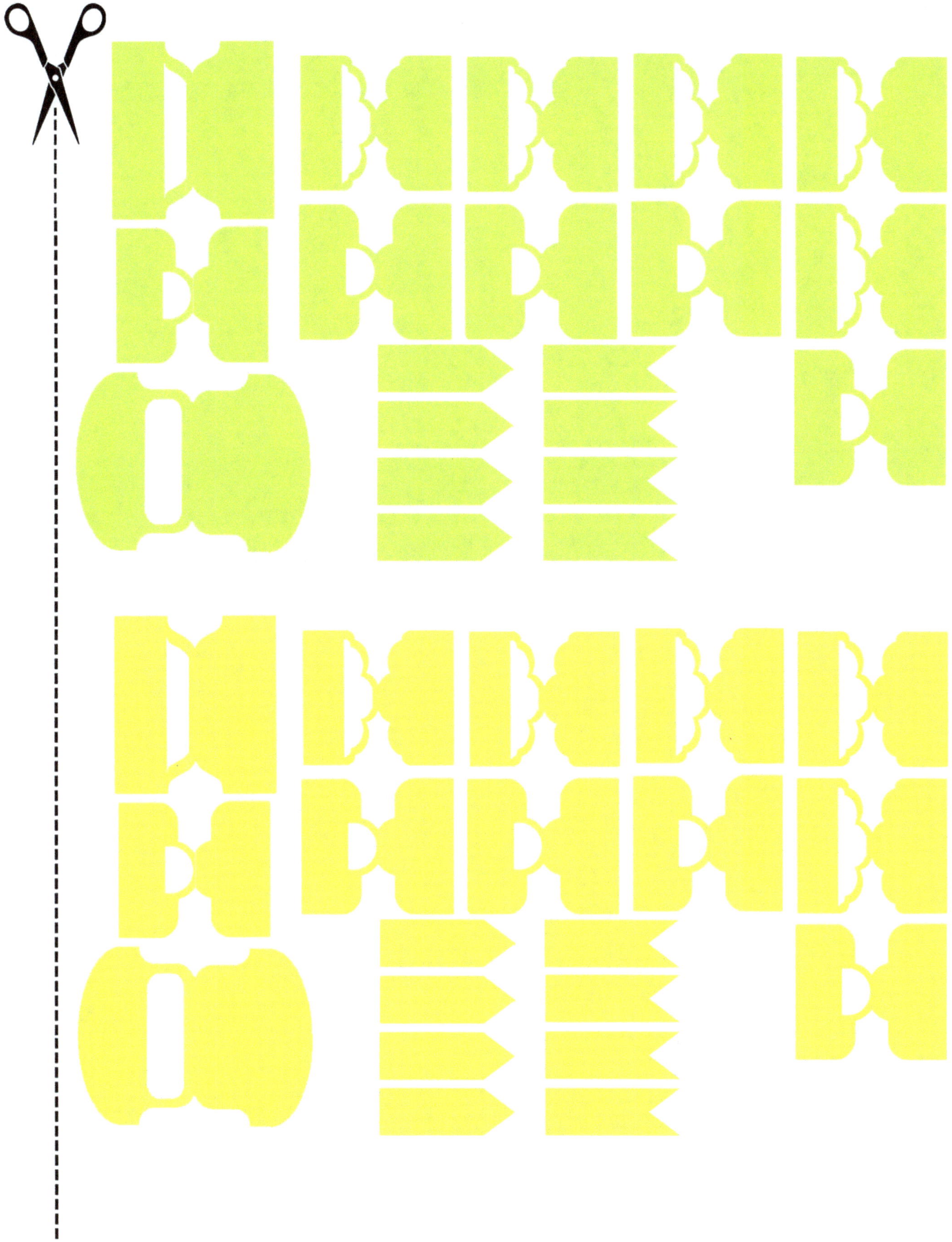

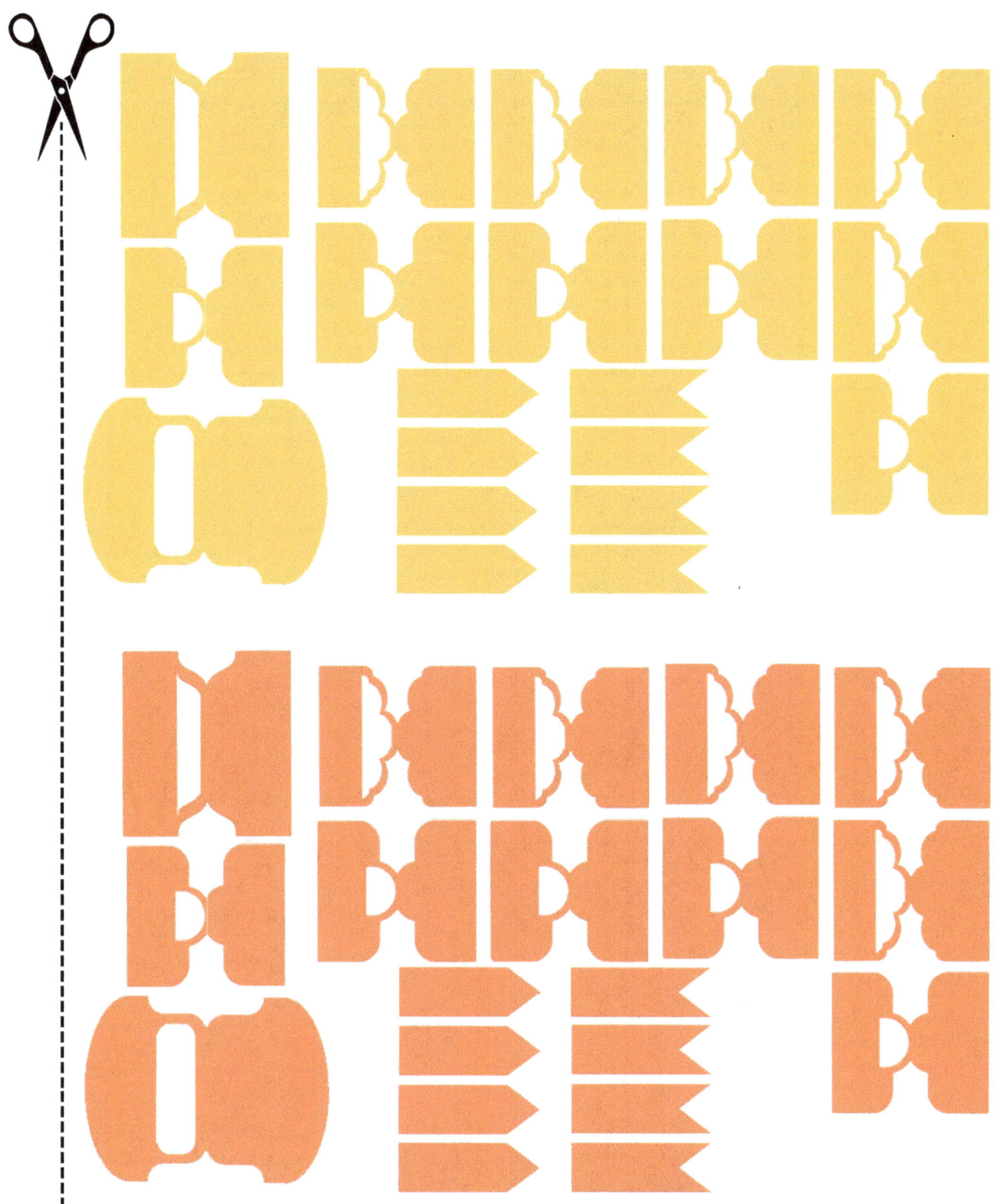

www.ingramcontent.com/pod-product-compliance
Lightning Source LLC
Chambersburg PA
CBHW082105090726
47910CB00009B/2603

* 9 7 8 0 9 9 5 0 1 2 9 2 9 *